WHERE MOUNTAINY MEN HAVE SOWN

War and Peace in Rebel Cork in the Turbulent Years 1916–21

Micheál Ó Súilleabháin

MERCIER PRESS

MERCIER PRESS

Cork

www.mercierpress.ie

© Estate of Micheál Ó Súilleabháin, 2013

ISBN: 978 1 78117 148 6

10 9 8 7 6 5 4 3 2

A CIP record for this title is available from the British Library

Printed and bound in the EU.

CONTENTS

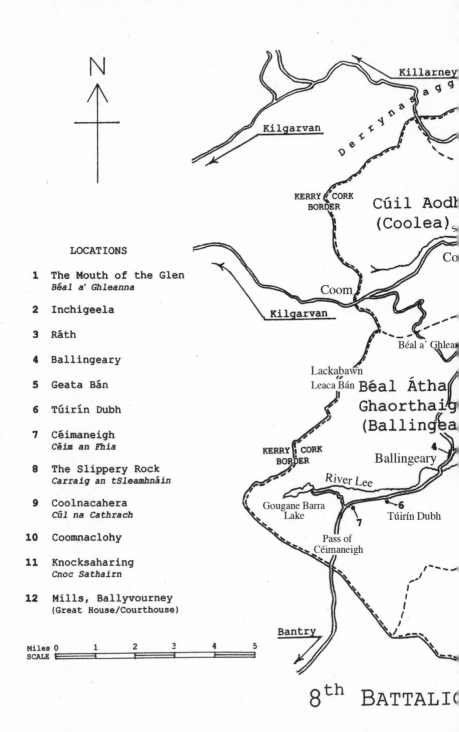

N

LOCATIONS

1 **The Mouth of the Glen**
  Béal a' Ghleanna

2 **Inchigeela**

3 **Ráth**

4 **Ballingeary**

5 **Geata Bán**

6 **Túirín Dubh**

7 **Céimaneigh**
  Céim an Fhia

8 **The Slippery Rock**
  Carraig an tSleamhnáin

9 **Coolnacahera**
  Cúl na Cathrach

10 **Coomnaclohy**

11 **Knocksaharing**
  Cnoc Sathairn

12 **Mills, Ballyvourney**
  (Great House/Courthouse)

Miles 0   1   2   3   4   5
SCALE

Killarney

Derrynasagg

Kilgarvan

KERRY / CORK
BORDER

Cúil Aodh
(Coolea)

Co

Coom

Kilgarvan

Béal a' Ghlea

Lackabawn
Leaca Bán Béal Átha
Ghaorthai
(Ballingea

KERRY | CORK
BORDER

Ballingeary

River Lee

Gougane Barra
Lake

Túirín Dubh

Pass of
Céimaneigh

Bantry

8th BATTALIO

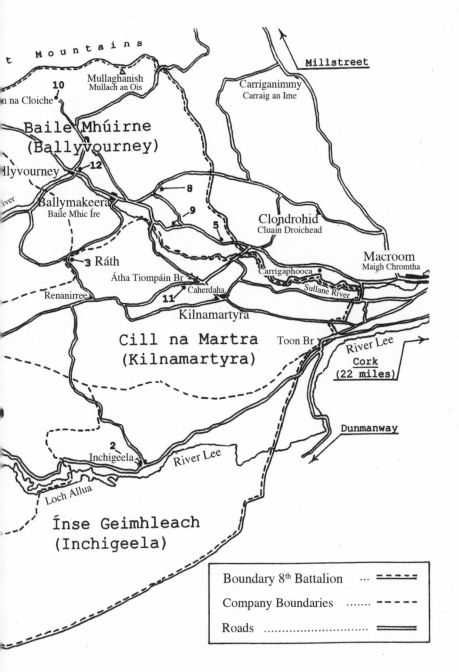

Mountains

Mullaghanish
Mullach an Ois

10

n na Cloiche

Millstreet

Carriganimmy
Carraig an Ime

Baile Mhúirne
(Ballyvourney)

llyvourney

12

iver

Ballymakeera
Baile Mhic Íre

8

9

5

Clondrohid
Cluain Droichead

3 Ráth

Átha Tiompáin Br

Renanirree

11

Caherdaha

Carrigaphooca

Macroom
Maigh Chromtha

Sullane River

Kilnamartyra

Cill na Martra
(Kilnamartyra)

Toon Br

River Lee

Cork
(22 miles)

Dunmanway

2

Inchigeela

River Lee

Loch Allua

Ínse Geimhleach
(Inchigeela)

Boundary 8th Battalion ···	=====
Company Boundaries ·······	-----
Roads	===

(1st CORK BRIGADE) AREA

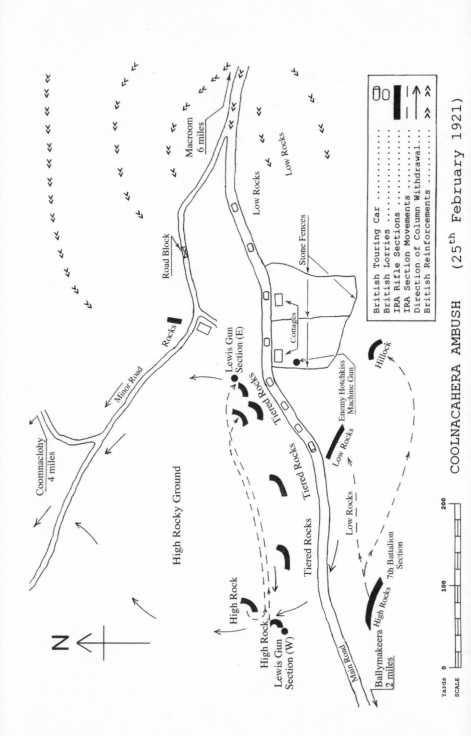

COOLNACAHERA AMBUSH (25th February 1921)

Key:
British Touring Car ....
British Lorries ....
IRA Rifle Sections ....
IRA Section Movements ....
Direction of Column Withdrawal..
British Reinforcements ....

Coomaclohy 4 miles

Macroom 6 miles

Minor Road

Road Block

Rocks

High Rocky Ground

Lewis Gun Section (E)

Tiered Rocks

Low Rocks

Low Rocks

Stone Fences

Cottages

Enemy Hotchkiss Machine Gun

Hillock

Tiered Rocks

Low Rocks

Tiered Rocks

Low Rocks

High Rock

High Rock

Lewis Gun Section (W)

Tiered Rocks

Main Road

Ballymakeera High Rocks 2 miles

7th Battalion Section

N

Yards 0   100   200
SCALE

INTRODUCTION

Micheál Ó Súilleabháin was born in 1902 in Cill na Martra (Kilnamartyra), County Cork. He was educated at primary level at Réidh na nDoirí National School, where his father and mother taught, and later at Rockwell College, County Tipperary. He joined the Volunteers at the age of thirteen and paraded with the Kilnamartyra Company on Easter Sunday 1916. Later he became engineer officer of the 8th Battalion, 1st Cork Brigade, and Lewis gunner for the battalion column. While still in his teens he took part in many raids and ambushes against the British forces.

He fought on the Republican side in the tragic Civil War, and though very badly wounded, survived and lived a long, happy life with his wife Máire (Máire Ní Shuibhne, Múirneach Beag, sister of Éamon Mac Suibhne, captain of Coolea Company), two sons and two daughters in an idyllic location at *Eas Coille*, Baile Mhúirne, County Cork.

He was a gifted storyteller and his tales, as well as being true to the facts, were always full of humour and amusing insights. His interest in culture was essentially global in its range, with a particular interest in literature and history. Having spent some years in Paris in the 1920s, he enjoyed the artistic riches of that city and also learned the language.

Perhaps his greatest interest and genius was as an engineer and inventor, notable by the choice of site where he settled in 1940, which included a cascading river that enabled him to build a hydro-electric scheme to power his new home and much-used workshop. When asked why he had not restored an existing ruined gazebo used by the former landlord, he quoted from a Bastille memorial plaque and said the remnants were incorporated into the foundations of a patio and stairs so that they might be forever trodden underfoot by a free people.

Although out of print, for many years his book has been reading material in the history departments of universities worldwide. Micheál wished to give a true account of events and though the book is a personal narrative, he consulted with many former comrades to ensure its authenticity. It is a story that comes to life as one reads it. Having grown up in the main geographic area in which the story is set, as described in the opening chapter, it becomes clear that the author has an intimate knowledge of that landscape and its people, customs and culture (including the songs, poems and stories of the locality), which would be difficult, if not impossible, for someone not of the area to effectively describe.

Where Mountainy Men Have Sown gives a unique insight to modern readers of a momentous period in Irish history.

Máire Ní Shúilleabháin & Tadhg Mac Suibhne

1

THE LITTLE FIELDS

If you journey westward along the valley of the River Lee from Cork city you see on either hand, in the main, a pleasant and fertile land. It is a hilly country, but not such as to hinder cultivation of the hills. This cultivation adds beauty to the landscape, especially in the harvest of the year. What vista can excel one of hillsides with the green of grass and gold of ripening grain? For twenty-four miles the scene unrolls itself before you, until the town of Macroom is reached. Here the vista ends.

West of Macroom is a new countryside, a more forbidding one. Rocks begin to uncover themselves, sleepy fellows on outpost duty. Before you have advanced many miles, however, you will have discovered that somehow they have managed to warn the main body. You will not wonder at this, when you see all their connecting files and advance guard. Ill-kept and ill-mannered fellows they look, peering at you from behind their cover of brushwood or furze, and some standing naked and unashamed in the middle of small fields on steep hillsides. But they are not bad fellows after all, and when you get to know them you will like them very much. Personally I have a grievance against some of them, for I live amongst them. So have my neighbours, for these stubborn fellows are forever coming in one's way. Yet they have their uses. And you must admire them for they are solid and unyielding, and the people who live with them must also acquire those qualities.

Let us continue our tour south-westward from Macroom into the country about which all these stories are told. We cross the Toon river by the bridge of the main road to Bantry and Glengariff. We are still on the northern bank of the Lee. We pass through Inchigeela village and now the Lee has widened and levelled to form Loch Allua, which in places almost laps the road, until we come to Ballingeary, five miles further on. Passing through this village of the Gaeltacht, we cross the bridge over the now narrow Lee, and continue westwards along its southern bank. Through a rugged glen with the cascading Lee as companion for a while, we go upwards through Túirín Dubh and soon the Pass of Céima-neigh confronts us. We will not go through that gap. We will look back for thirteen miles to Toon bridge. Thirteen miles of rugged scenery with a lake and two villages. Little pockets of green fields set, high and low, among the overwhelm-ing rocks, marshes and bogs. Those thirteen miles form the southern boundary of the area I write about.

We will turn north and climb to Gougane Barra where rises the Lee. Once the abode of a saint (Finbarr), it is well known for its beauty, the little lake and island set in a corridor of towering and barren rocks. I would say that it is the general headquarters for all the rocks in that district. To traverse the western boundary of our area we must now go on foot across the Derrynasaggart mountains, travelling north by east until we reach the first east–west road crossing at Lackabawn. Again roughly north until we meet the next at Coom (the Cork–Kenmare road) and finally north by east again to meet the Cork–Killarney road at the Cork–Kerry border. We have completed a further ten miles, the extent of our western boundary. It is a mountain wall, heather-covered in places, barren enough in the remainder. Some feeding for small mountain sheep. Some peat bogs. Cover for grouse now, it was once the home of the eagle. From heights of over a thousand feet one may look down to the east and see nearly all our territory spread before him. The two principal rivers, the Lee and the Sullane, form with their valleys the whole of the ground we wish to cover.

Moving due east along the ridge of the Derrynasaggart mountains, we follow the mountain road between Ballyvourney and Millstreet for a few miles as far as the source of the Foherish. Three further miles eastward and we have completed our northern boundary, roughly six miles.

Turning due south with the rocky Foherish we reach

Carrigaphooca, where the Foherish joins the Sullane, which comes from the western boundary. Here we cross the Sullane, a few miles to the west of Macroom, and continuing due south over a dividing ridge reach the Toon river at Toon bridge, the place from whence we started. The circuit of our area is complete. We have enclosed perhaps a hundred square miles and three parishes, Inchigeela–Ballingeary, Ballyvourney and Kilnamartyra.

What of the physical features within the enclosure? They are in keeping with the boundaries. Massive ridges of rock run from west to east through the entire area. There are not twenty acres together in any part of it, in which a rock, large or small, does not show. A twenty-acre field even with a rock showing is indeed a rarity. And small level fields are rare enough. The vast majority are inclined at a more or less difficult angle to the horizontal. All have been reclaimed from the rock, the marsh, the bog, the heather, the brake, and, worst of all, from the stony and eroded hillside. The quality of the soil is not good, even in the best pockets. I have seen little fields, reclaimed by past generations, where the area under the stone fence around one field exceeded one quarter of the area of the field itself. This was due, of course, to the number and depth of stones and boulders that had to be removed from the reclaimed area. A horse and cart could be driven on top of some of these fences. The little fields and big fences were indeed made at the cost of blood and sweat and tears.

What of the people who made the little fields? The best on earth, I would say. Driven long ago from the fertile inland by successive plantations, they took root among the rocks. It is significant that all bear old Irish names. You will rarely find a Planter's name among them. If you do you will find that it is located on a spot worth occupying. It is hard to visualise how any human being, no matter how strong and courageous, survived the winters before the first little field was made. One could build a house of some sort in a short time, but to make a field in the wilderness takes time and energy. Food must be had to provide the energy. However, it was certainly done and the green spots started to show against the dour and forbidding background. In time, and following a colossal expenditure of human tissue and with the worst of tools, the little fields and cabin showed signs of the owner's industry. They caught the Planter's eye.

Surely the man who starts to work on a piece of rejected raw material and makes some useful article from it is entitled to be recognised as the lawful owner of it? Surely the unfortunate people who had to comply with the order 'to Hell or Connaught' were entitled to call the rocks their own? They had just been forced out of the good land they lawfully owned to make room for the Planters. To go to Connaught meant to go to the waste places where they could suffer and die at their leisure. The majority did die, but some survived and started to make the little fields. Surely the raw material they used belonged to them? It was flung at them as an alternative to hell. Certainly it was the next thing to it.

Now having made homes of a sort from hell's alternative, the tormented people expected that at least their right to the meagre fruits of their labour would not be disputed. But the greedy Sassenach eye saw a way further to persecute the mere Irish and at the same time to enrich himself.

The rocks were divided into estates. A man's mud-wall cabin and little fields were classified as 'holdings' and 'farms', and groups of them became estates 'belonging' to a landlord who already lived in the home of some Irishman driven to the rocks. Some there were who never saw 'their estates' but lived in England or elsewhere. They employed agents who collected the rents from the tenants. Thus did the people come to know those hated terms.

As well as taking rents from the people, the landlord 'owned' their bodies and tried hard for the mastery of their souls. If he wanted a man or men or women, he merely sent a servant intimating the time and place where his or their services were required. He 'owned' the wild birds of the air and all the ground game. Woe to the man or boy caught chasing a hare or setting a trap or snare. The penalty was meted out according to the humour of the particular land-lord, he being also the local dispenser of British justice. I can cite an instance, from living witnesses, where the landlord's gamekeeper saw a young man crossing one of the Derrynasaggart mountains accompanied by a greyhound. He shot the young man with a rifle and killed him. The gamekeeper was never brought to trial before a court. He left the country and there the matter ended. I am happy to relate, however, that some spirited young men from the parish of Ballyvourney crossed the Kerry border and, driving the landlord's men before them into the Big House, they laid siege to it. A strong party of armed police soon intervened to effect a timely rescue.

My uncle, Dan Harrington, often told me of a little incident, which reveals an honest Englishman's opinion of both the integrity of the landlord and the quality of the land he lorded over. One day when about twelve years old, Dan met a landlord and party shooting woodcock. Anxious to see this, for him, unusual pastime, he stood on a rock to watch the proceedings. The game was plentiful and his point of vantage being excellent he stayed on it. Presently the landlord and one of his guests, a British Army captain, also mounted the rock to rest and survey the activities of their companions. The captain's eyes ranged over the terrain. At length he spoke.

'Sir Augustus,' he said, 'did I hear you say that you took rents from the people about here?'

'Oh, yes,' replied Sir Augustus Warren, 'the land about here is very good.'

'Good,' exclaimed the captain in astonishment. 'Good!'

'Egad sir, it is, for *cock shooting*!'

The forces of nature arrayed against the people were indeed formidable and unrelenting. My father told me how the little fields were made. Having cleared an area which had disputed every inch with them, the people could not afford to relax their heart-breaking toil and vigilance to any extent. For the nature of the soil was such that its desire to return to its former state was unappeasable. Like a genuine wild creature it was untameable. Did one but turn one's back on it for but a short time, the rushes and the furze and the heather appeared above its surface. Even the rock that had been passed over 'grew' again. I remember an old man's comment on the reclamation of a particularly boulder-infested patch. He stood watching the crowbar work for a while and then, referring to the soil, said, 'It is hard. Do ye think ye will be able to *release* it?' Yet there was little soil to release compared with the volume of stone.

The other forces massed against the people since, let us say, the year after the battle of Kinsale in 1601, were the alien forces that had driven them to the rocks. On the first day of the new year, 1603, O'Sullivan Beare, the last Irish military leader to tread the land, passed northwards through Ballingeary, Kilnamartyra and Ballyvourney on his last fiery trail into history. Military resistance, for the old Irish, was finished for many a weary year to come. Wars there were that helped in the further destruction of the natives and the confiscation of their lands. But they were wars between English rulers and it mattered little to the people which gained the mastery. Men like Eoghain Rua O'Neill and Sarsfield wasted their lives and talents fighting for Charles I and Seamus a' chaca. It was not until the year 1798 that a serious attempt was made to shake off the yoke of the foreigner. It was a military failure, yet it was a victory in every other way. It showed the people, the enemy and the world that the utmost repression and barbarity of penal laws could not, though maintained for centuries, bring the people to their knees. Sir John Moore of Corunna, humane and gallant British soldier, who witnessed the brutalities of the soldiery and yeomanry of '98, exclaimed: 'If I were an Irishman, I would be a rebel.' His own people did not appreciate his humanity, but Michael O'Dwyer of Wicklow did when he released him after capture, and Soult, Marshal of France, paid him tribute by erecting a monument over his grave at Corunna.

The year 1803 saw Emmet's attempt to throttle British power at its source in Dublin. Its failure was succeeded by the usual intensified crushing of body and spirit.

The year 1602 had also seen the end of the Irish system of laws which had functioned for fifteen hundred years. They were replaced by a penal system, every modification of which was intended to improve on or supplant some feature thought to be over-merciful to the people. One of the most hated enactments was the Tithe Law, which made it compulsory on the people, almost entirely Catholic, to pay one-tenth of their meagre means of subsistence towards the support of an alien Church.

The people of our area were always ready to grasp at any opportunity to assert their rights by force of arms. In 1796 they heard of the coming of the French fleet to Bantry bay to aid them and grasped the poor arms they possessed. They were well watched, however, by the combined forces of the regular army and yeomanry of the Barony of Muskerry. This yeomanry force was composed entirely of Planters and captained by landlords. They were dressed in uniform and were well armed with sword, pistol and carbine. The French fleet under Hoche was unable to land troops because of fierce and prolonged gales, and had to put to sea again. Máire Bhuí Ní Laoghaire, a local poet, in her poem *Ar Leacain na Gréine* laments the failure of the French to land:

> Tháinig scaipeadh ortha ón ngaoith, foríor! chuir a lán acu ar strae
> Agus i nglasaibh 'seadh do shuidhid mar an righbean seo thárlaidh a gcéin.

In the year 1822, our people took up arms again. Poor weapons they had, pikes and old, unreliable muskets. They refused to pay the tithe rent and prepared to resist as best they could. As a preliminary they decided to raid for arms the Big Houses of the Planters in the neighbourhood of Bantry town. While engaged in this enterprise, word was conveyed to the military authorities in both Bantry and Macroom. At that time a company of the Rifle Brigade occupied barracks in Inchigeela. All took the field, the Muskerry and Bantry yeomen included, and proceeded to round up our men who had just reached their own area south of the Pass of Céimaneigh. They had scattered among the houses of Túirín na nÉan, Cloch Barrach and Na hÍnseacha at the foot of Dúchoill mountain. They reassembled and took up a position to the south of the old Cork–Bantry road. As soldiers and yeomen coming from the east and west deployed in front of them, they opened fire. The enemy took cover and our men followed up with bayonet and pike to meet a volley which killed two of their number, Amhlaoibh Ó Luingsigh from Doireach (in the parish of Kilnamartyra) and Barra Ó Laoghaire from Gaortha na Tornóra (in the parish of Ballingeary).

In the hand-to-hand fight which followed, a British soldier was killed. His name was John Smith, of the Rifle Brigade. The entire enemy force broke and fled for their lives. Our men took away their dead. Amhlaoibh Ó Luingsigh was buried in Ballyvourney, and Barra Ó Laoghaire in the old graveyard in Inchigeela. They buried the soldier

Smith in Muing na Biorraí at Gort Luachra. Later he was transferred to the old graveyard in Inchigeela, where a stone erected by his comrades marks his grave.

Máire Bhuí witnessed the battle. One of her brothers fought in it. She composed a poem which, although the engagement itself was relatively small, will keep its memory alive while the Irish language lives. It tells of the peace of the countryside, of how happy she was as she listened to the singing of the birds. Then suddenly the dreadful sound of an army approaching came to her ears. The heavy harmony of the cavalry and the general vibration of the whole army seemed to shake the mountain. The terror of the women and children as they ran from their homes bewailing the fate of their fathers, brothers and husbands who they thought would be encircled and whose utter destruction seemed imminent. The sight of other brave men hurrying to the scene to help their neighbours or die with them. The rolling volleys of musketry. The fierce charge with the steel of our men. The immediate break and utter rout of the well-equipped and numerically far superior enemy. The joy at the seemingly impossible victory. The praise for her great men of the Gael. The return of hope. The exhortation to stand firm with the good steel always ready. The vision of the day when Irishmen would be back in the good land of Ireland which they had had to yield. The final verse where she admitted harbouring a good deal of ill-feeling for the pot-bellied Planters. She would say no more about them, but would merely pray that slaughter and the terror of rout might attend on them.

The Famine of 1847 did not begin or end in that year. A state of semi-starvation already existed. It is true that the failure of the potato crop in that year precipitated it. But there was no actual shortage of food anywhere – better food than the potato. The fact was that *all* the grain grown by the small farmer went to pay the rents, the landlord's and the tithe rents. The failure of the potato crop wrung no concession from the landlord. The rents had to be paid. Where the grain was not sold to pay the rents it was seized on the field under armed protection. It is a fact that even grain for seed for the coming year was seized. Thus it came about that the rent could not, willingly or otherwise, be paid on the following year. If the tenant had not already left his home, the 'notice to quit' was served on him. Then the crowbar and the battering-ram laid his cabin in ruin. He and his family were thrown on the roadside to die. It was convenient for the landlord in any case. A drop in the price of corn in Britain due to free import from other countries, and a good market for meat there decided the question. Now he would get rid of those troublesome human cattle and keep bullocks and sheep instead. And so it happened. The great exodus started. Some, who left in time, reached America. Some died on the coffin ships. Some died by the wayside.

How fared the people of our area during this period of artificial famine? People died of hunger here as well as in other places, but not to the same extent. This was due to the fact that the people shared their meagre supplies of oatmeal with stranger or neighbour who wanted it. Many of them defended their grain crops. The battle of Céimaneigh, fought in 1822, now repaid them for the losses suffered there. For besides reducing the tithe and landlord rents, it showed tyrants who might consider further oppression the danger of pressing such people too far. Again, eviction of the people would ill-profit the landlord, for the little fields would return to the mountain state in a short time.

At all times, the people deemed it an honour to give food and shelter to men who strove or had striven to free Ireland. Big rewards for information leading to the capture of such men left them unmoved, or rather spurred them to further efforts to ensure their safety. Treachery was unknown among them. Michael Doheny, one of the leaders of the 1848 insurrection, came among them after that failure. He speaks highly of their generosity at a time when they themselves had little to give. In his poem, 'The Felon's Track', he says:

Hurrah for the scanty meal
When served by ungrudging hand,
Hurrah for the hearts of steel
Still true to a fallen land.

And in his poem, 'A Cuisle Geal Mo Chroidhe', he mentions the treatment he received from the rich, who lived on the fat of the land. Speaking of the Ireland of his love, he says:

> For thee I've tracked the mountain's sides,
> And slept within the brake,
> More lonely than the swan that glides,
> O'er Lua's fairy lake.
> The rich have spurned me from their door,
> Because I'd make thee free:
> Yet still I love thee all the more,
> *A cuisle geal mo Chroidhe!*

Among the many and varied devices resorted to for keeping the people in slavery was the effective one of keeping them uneducated. Not until 1831 were the penal laws against education for the Irish relaxed. Not alone was it a felony for the Old Irish to teach or be taught in Ireland, but it was a crime to send a child to school abroad. Under these terrible conditions the hedge-schoolmaster or 'poor scholar' was the man in the gap. He had been so since the battle of Kinsale. The hedge-schoolmaster was a survival of the ancient Bardic professional schools. The Bards, who were poets as well as scholars, were classed next to royalty.

The hedge-schoolmaster, often educated abroad, taught

by the sheltered side of a fence in summer. In winter the school was indoors in some old cabin. The children brought sods of turf each day for the fire, as well as bottles of home-made ink and quill pens. They sat on planks mounted on stones and wrote on their knees. The subjects taught were Irish, English, Greek, Latin, Mathematics and Natural Philosophy. The teacher was paid, as best they could, by the people whose children he taught. Padraig Colum, the poet, gives a description of the teachers' difficulties:

> My eyelids red and heavy are,
> With bending o'er the smouldering peat,
> I know the Aeneid now by heart,
> My Virgil read in cold and heat,
> In loneliness and hunger smart.
> And I know Homer, too, I ween,
> As Munster poets know Ossian.

Evidently he must have reprimanded one of his students of the 'forties' for inattention, for:

> You teach Greek verbs and Latin nouns,
> The dreamer of Young Ireland said.
> You do not hear the muffled call,
> The sword being forged, the far-off tread
> Of hosts to meet as Gael and Gall –

What good to us your wisdom store,
Your Latin verse, your Grecian lore?

Along with the Bardic schools of ancient Ireland went the courts of poetry, where the Bards met from time to time and conducted their proceedings entirely through the medium of classical Gaelic poetry. One of these still survives at Coolea, in the parish of Ballyvourney. It holds annual session on the sixth day of January. The poets of our area can hold their own against the best in Ireland and are the true successors of the Bards.

The rugged splendour of the rocks, the falling water, the encircling mountains and the solitude attracted Anglo-Irish poets as well as the Bards. The most notable was Jeremiah Joseph Callanan (1795–1829). A student of Maynooth and Trinity College, he spent some years among the people here collecting a store of legendary lore, and became a rebel himself. 'Gougane Barra' is one of his best poems:

Least bard of the hills! were it mine to inherit
The fire of thy harp, and the wing of thy spirit,
With the wrongs which like thee to our country have bound me,
Did your mantle of song fling its radiance around me,
Still, still in those wilds might young liberty rally,
And send her strong shout over mountain and valley,
The star of the west might yet rise in its glory,
And the land that was darkest be brightest in story.

The Fenian rising in 1867 was the last organised military effort on a national scale before our time. For some time before and for many years after '67, the organisation was maintained in our area. It resulted in a long term in jail and finally exile for one of my uncles. Police searches for suspects, raids for arms, arrests and trials had become of almost daily occurrence. The people got quite accustomed to them. There would never be peace in any case. In the event of a short period of inactivity, the landlord came to the conclusion that he was losing money, that the tenants were getting prosperous, that it was time to raise the rent. The raising of the rent was but the prelude to the raising of troubles. Notices, refusals, seizures or attempted seizures of cattle, rescues, clashes with bailiffs and police, kept the times generally up to quite a high standard of excitement.

In 1879 Michael Davitt founded the Land League to demand the return of the land to the people. The people, *en masse*, joined the League. Never before in Ireland had there been such complete unanimity of demand. Evictions, imprisonment and buckshot made not the slightest impression on the determination of the League. At last a series of Land Acts was wrenched from the British Parliament. The little fields came back to those who had made them. Davitt had planned for this victory during long years of solitary confinement in Dartmoor prison. The people had cause to be thankful to him. I have heard him called 'the Greatest of them all'. Only for the Land League victory, the success of later activities would not have been possible.

One would think that the never-ending struggle of the people against the forces of nature and the injustice of man would eventually bring them to look on life with a bitter eye. But such was not the case. They never lost their gaiety of manner. They examined defeat until finally they found some humour among its ruins. Then they laughed mightily and set about building up again. One would think that, having grown up among the rocky hills and tasted of their hardness, it would be too difficult for them to think kindly of them. But the reverse is the case. The rocky hills have, from time immemorial, proved a refuge from total extinction for the Irish race. Were it not for them and their strong sheltering arms always outstretched to help the weary forces of the Gael, the unequal struggle could not be maintained. And having sheltered the weary, they again induce the spirit of freedom in them. For who, standing on their breezy summits, and gazing towards limitless horizons can take the short, or small, or mean view of anything? One of the beauties of the world, is, according to Pádraig Pearse:

Some quiet hill where mountainy man hath sown,
And soon would reap; near to the gate of Heaven.

2

THE START

I was born in 1902, the year the Boer war ended. It was the first war I heard discussed when I began to understand things a little.

Indeed when I push my memory back as far as possible, I always reach the one definite point. I can see my uncle, Dan Harrington, in front of the fire, Tom Connor on his right, my father on his left. My mother generally moving about, forever busy, like all good mothers. At length the men would prevail on her to sit down.

'Yerra, Mini, sit down, the world will be after us,' Tom would say. Then would we all, my brothers and sisters, listen entranced to good stories. I heard for the first time the names of famous Boer leaders, Kruger, Cronje, De Wett, De La Rey and others, and of Mauser, Maxim, Pom-pom and Long Tom.

Persistent enquiries from the younger generation were made until we had a fair grasp of the meaning of all these people and things. Then did we really enjoy the story of the successful fight of the weak against the strong. The stories about the Boer war never grew old in my youth. Any dog worthy of the name was called Kruger, pronounced Kroojer. Jerry Kelleher, Ballyvoig, was the only exception. In order to be contrary, he had a dog named Balfour. When the crows at his heels, while Jerry scattered grain in the tillage, got too numerous and clamorous, Jerry would say to the dog, 'Disperse those meetings, Mr Balfour.' Balfour always obliged.

The stories of, and the discussions on, the Boer war never ended without a reference to Ireland. Small wonder. The handful of farmers who stood up against an empire, and humiliated it, set an example for the oppressed and downtrodden of the world. The example was not lost on the militant-minded in our own country. My uncle was one of these and it was from him I first heard of the only sure way to shake off the foreign oppressor. For years before I heard of Sinn Féin I heard its gospel from him, but above all I learned that the only way to freedom was the direct way. When Home Rule or Westminster or Irish Party or a 'great speech' was mentioned, he sat up and ejaculated: 'Hah! Stinking politicians.' Too young to have been a Fenian, he had a brother Mike who spent eleven months in Limerick jail for illegal drilling, in an effort to carry on the Fenian organisation. (My uncle Dan, Dan Harrington, and the 'Farmer' are one and the same person throughout this story.)

Around the fire we learned the history of our own and other countries. That was before the kitchens of Ireland became afflicted with the television and the radio. Then would we hear an honest man's opinion or his hearty laugh, or listen to the stories handed down to him from his forefathers and told in the same way around the unquenchable fire.

The stories around the fire were not always told in prose. Any influx of the neighbours brought some one or more able to sing. Thus did we hear every national song or ballad worth singing. At that time people of each small district met often and worked and played together. On a Sunday there was the *Patron* in the summer, or a bowling match or football game. During the long nights, the *scoruiacht*, where all the neighbours met at one house until about ten o'clock. In the harvest, the threshing dance each night a haggard was threshed. Never did I attend one of these functions where songs alternated with dances without hearing a national song expressing the peoples' hope that one day they would see Ireland free.

My father, a member of the Gaelic League, always attended the Oireachtas. He knew Father O'Growney and Pádraig Pearse. He and my mother went out on a tender from Cobh to meet O'Growney's funeral from Los Angeles in 1903. Both O'Growney and Rooney worked like Pearse, but death intervened before they saw The Day. They had worn themselves out early in life working almost alone at the stupendous task of regenerating the soul of Ireland. With a few others, they must be regarded as the apostles of both the separatist movement and the language revival. Another man who did not live to see The Day was William Bulfin, but he knew it was not far off. His one book, *Rambles in Eirinn*, helped a great deal to teach self-respect to Irishmen and may profitably be read in these times, when we hear of Irishmen fighting as mercenaries. Here and now I must say that every effort should be made from school, platform and pulpit, to point out to young men the immorality and disgrace of fighting in foreign armies. I think the name 'the fighting Irish' the greatest insult ever offered to our race. It implies that we fight just for the fun of it. Alas for the poor lads who died in the Tugela valley fighting against the Boers, against Zulus and other weak people. If only they had fought for those oppressed peoples, 'Their graves we would keep where the Fenians sleep.' And that brings me to the greatest slaughter of our young men in the service of Britain, during the world war of 1914–1918.

The politicians, whom my uncle used to describe so aptly, were the cause of the slaughter. These traffickers in blood, who maintained that 'the floor of the House' was the place to win Irish independence, shamelessly sent the youth of Ireland to the shambles. The unfortunate people had been bewildered for a long time previously. A Home Rule Bill was dangled before them as 'independence'. Carson's threat to resist it with his Ulster Volunteers gave Irishmen the opportunity of forming the National Volunteers, ostensibly to oppose Carson.[1] In reality, the National Volunteers were established by the Irish Republican Brotherhood, who saw the opportunity for arming and drilling a body of men to fight for the complete independence of Ireland. As this body grew in strength, Redmond, leader of the Irish Party in Westminster, demanded representation on its committee. This was granted to him and the numerical strength of the National Volunteers increased tenfold. On the outbreak of the world war in the beginning of August 1914, Redmond offered them body and soul to Britain. Moreover, he started a recruiting campaign throughout the country, and, aided by the daily press and his own party organisation, together with lying propaganda, soon reaped a red harvest. Thousands volunteered and, as was always the case, many found graves in the front line of Britain's battlefields. Poor lads, they thought they were dying for Ireland.

I have said that the National Volunteers, or Redmond's Volunteers as they were called, became very strong numerically when the political party gained control. Age or youth were not considered in enlistment. I was myself a member

---

1   *Publisher's Note:* The organisation formed to oppose the Ulster Volunteers was known as the Irish Volunteers. It was only when the organisation split in 1914 that the majority part led by John Redmond became known as the National Volunteers, the minority keeping the name Irish Volunteers.

at the age of thirteen. We looked an imposing body in the dusk of the evening when viewed from a considerable distance. My comrade-in-arms was a Mr Twomey, a prosperous farmer of about sixty years. He showed his prosperity around his waist and should have started his military career as a general. We drilled nearly every evening and had a sergeant major of the Irish Guards Regiment of the British Army as instructor. A splendid instructor he was, and if he had had the necessary material would quickly have made soldiers of us. He had my great sympathy.

Thus we drilled and paraded for a time, about one hundred strong. Then one evening twenty men, my uncle, brother and myself included, stood apart. We were the Irish Volunteers, later to become known as the Irish Republican Army. The remainder continued to soldier on for some little time. One Sunday morning they paraded with their band. The local committee spokesman announced that their destination was a recruiting meeting in Macroom. The band struck up a martial air and moved off on hearing the command. The National Volunteers did not stir. When they moved again it was to disperse and go home never to assemble again. The big drummer of the band looked back, stopped, unbuckled his drum and let it roll down the hill. Excepting the local spokesman, no one went to the meeting.

Nothing daunted, this local prop of empire announced an after-Mass recruiting meeting for a certain Sunday. A doctor from Macroom, a Clerk of the Crown and Peace from Cork, a British Army captain, a recruiting sergeant and an army piper awaited the people outside the chapel gates. The people stood around and waited while the piper played some warlike music. The visitors hoped that perhaps the Parish Priest, Father O'Donohue, might preside at the meeting. He came striding down to the gate, a tall imperious man. Two approached him just outside the gate, but he brushed them aside with a contemptuous gesture of his hand and walked quickly home without looking back. The local prop of empire introduced them himself. An audible silence persisted. Then up stood the Clerk of the Crown and Peace and told of the atrocities of the Huns and introduced the captain who had slain legions of them. The captain held up a captured German rifle for inspection. He told how the Germans came in waves, in masses. He and his comrades mowed them down, but still they came. When he was leaving they were coming stronger than ever. I thought it a very poor inducement to a prospective recruit.

Our Volunteer company had gone to exercise near Macroom that day. With three other locals I had contrived to stay for the meeting. The meeting was now over and nothing remained but to enrol the recruits. No one stepped forward, but one man hung around the piper as if fascinated by the pipes. This young man was a splendid player of the flute but never had handled the pipes. The recruiting sergeant approached and spoke to the young man whose name was Paddy. Finally the entire recruiting unit retired to the nearest pub, taking Paddy with them. Two of my comrades entered the pub to watch the proceedings. They returned with the news that Paddy had accepted the Saxon shilling. That was bad news. The four of us waited outside. Presently all appeared, with Paddy in their midst playing the pipes. A few pints of porter had dulled the voice of reason. The group repaired to the second pub in the village. More music and more porter.

At length they all emerged. They were going back to their base. Two motor cars stood ready. Paddy still clutched the pipes and made some attempt to play them. One of the group remarked: 'Ah well, we had not a very profitable day, only one recruit.' The doors were opened. All seated themselves except two. One held a door open while the other, the sergeant, took Paddy's arm saying: 'Step in, Paddy.'

Never did I see such horror on a man's face as I did on Paddy's. We stood with our backs to the wall of the pub. Paddy's eyes turned and looked at us appealingly. He was now quite sober. The shock had roused him to the danger of his position. I was the first to reach him. I grasped his arm and jerked him away from the sergeant. There were now five of us. The sergeant looked at us and said: 'He is our recruit. Do ye know what ye're doing?'

I answered for my comrades: 'Just now you had one recruit. Now you have no recruit. If you go further into the matter with us you will find that you may be minus more than recruits.'

The sergeant leaned over one of the cars. A whispered consultation and we were left the victors, with a new recruit who later proved himself a good soldier of the IRA. As they drove off, we could not forbear a derisive cheer.

The local company soon reached a strength of thirty men. They drilled regularly and exercised by night and day. Arms were sadly lacking. The shotgun loaded with buckshot was the only firearm. Across a road or street it was effective enough. Elsewhere it was not. Even the shotguns were scarce. To make good the deficiency, about twenty pikes were forged. Beautifully fashioned they were, by local tradesmen. Of little practical value, yet they showed the spirit of the men who bore them and demonstrated the desire to be free.

3

1916 AND AFTER

A few weeks before the Rising of 1916, my uncle, taking with him five Volunteers, raided the houses of everyone known to possess firearms in the district. He collected a large number of shotguns. He then proceeded to put his own house into a state of defence. It was a farmhouse where he lived alone and a mile distant from the village.

I visited him daily. Four or five armed Volunteers were with him night and day. Evidently he was waiting for something to happen. The windows were barricaded and shotguns lay on the tables, all loaded.

Sunday 23 April came. After first Mass the Company, each man armed with either a shotgun or a pike and carrying a full day's rations, left the village. We went the nearest way to Millstreet. At Carriganimma we halted. There came the news of the disaster in Kerry and of the coming from Germany of the *Aud*. We heard of how the arms ship, having successfully evaded the British blockade, reached Tralee bay. We heard of her long period of waiting for men who did not come to take the arms from her. We heard of the capture of the *Aud*, the landing and capture of Roger Casement, and the accidental drowning of the three Volunteers at Ballykissane pier. We returned home in bad spirits, my uncle especially so. We pitied him, since he had waited a long time for that day.

The following day we heard nothing. Next we heard newspaper accounts of the Rising, but nothing through Volunteer channels. My uncle still kept vigil with his small garrison. On Thursday he went to a funeral at Ballyvourney, four miles distant. He was not armed. A party of RIC arrested him and a Volunteer who accompanied him. Both were taken handcuffed in a motor car to Macroom. We heard the news at home. My brother ordered me off to my uncle's house at Knocksaharing and rushed out to mobilise some men of the Company.

When I reached the house, I found the key where my uncle always hid it. Then I found that the lock had been broken and when I went in I knew that the place had been raided by the police. Joe Roche, a Volunteer who worked for my uncle, now arrived. Joe explained to me how, before going to the funeral, they had removed all the guns from the house and dumped them temporarily. That was very satisfactory. We hurried back to the village.

Twelve men were now assembled under arms. My brother led us down the road towards Macroom. He had sent a Volunteer on a bicycle ahead to request the Macroom Company to hold the railway station. This they did. The police, aware of the move and having no car of their own available, asked a Protestant hotel-keeper for a car to drive the prisoners to Cork. He refused. They next asked the Catholic hotel-keeper. He drove the car himself. Thus it happened that halfway to Macroom a Volunteer cyclist met us with the news that my uncle and his comrade had already been taken away to Cork. Another disappointment. Had the miserable hotel-keeper refused the use of his car as the other decent man had done, and delayed the matter for half an hour, things would have been different.

We were, with the Macroom Volunteers, numerically superior to the RIC in the barracks there. Any attempt to remove the prisoners would have been doomed to failure had we arrived in time. Indeed, the attempt would have been very welcome to us, as it would mean their leaving the shelter of their barracks to face the shotguns in a narrow street.

After the removal of the prisoners it would appear that a few shoneen young men of the town repaired to the barracks and offered their services to defend the building against the Volunteers. We were later to meet and suitably reward them for their generous impulse.

My uncle saw the inside of many British gaols and

finally the camps of Frongoch. Christmas was over when he reached home again. His mother, my grandmother, was there to welcome him. She had been living at home with us, but when she heard of her son's arrest she insisted on going back to the old home and remaining there until he returned. She was very old and her time had come to die, but she insisted that she would live until Dan came home.

'When he comes home,' she used to say, 'then ye can carry me to Kilmurray.' I had stayed with her while Dan was away, and the house was often raided and searched by military and police. Very early in the morning they invariably came. From her bed in a room below she would call upstairs to me: 'Mick, you must come down to admit the *ragged regiment*!' This was a term of contempt for the forces of the crown in the land war.

She had seen famine, Fenians, evictions and emigration, and many were the stories I heard from her of the 'bad times'. My mother told me how once in a fight with police and bailiffs for possession of cattle in the yard of her home, my grandmother, then a young woman, took a decisive part. The men were being forced backwards. She rushed into the yard and, seizing an old cart by the two shafts, she pressed them apart. One gave way before the strength of her fury. Grasping it with both hands she rushed on the enemy. Her example carried the day.

I was present to witness her triumph at Dan's homecoming. 'Oh Dan,' she cried, 'I lived to see you home again. Now won't I be happy going to Kilmurray!'

She talked with us, my mother, my uncle and me, for a long time. Then she lay back smiling and said she would rest. We stole away to the kitchen. In the kitchen there was an old clock. Every week, she reminded me to wind it. 'Maybe we will have good news before it is wound again,' she would say.

Ellen Cronin, her nurse, returned to the bedroom again. Soon Ellen called softly to me. 'She is dying,' she said when I went with her.

'She is sleeping,' I said.

We knelt down. We could hear nothing but the gentle breathing and the measured tick of the old clock. Presently I noticed the breathing getting slower, but yet it seemed to me to keep harmony with the clock. Slower and slower, and fainter and fainter. Then – it stopped. And with it stopped the old clock. Old Ellen looked at me.

'The clock stopped,' she said.

'It did,' I answered.

We called my mother and my uncle in from the kitchen. They knelt down with us.

* * *

The new year, 1917, started quietly. A few Volunteers met at my uncle's house at least once a week and discussed the future. Now and again we opened dumps and cleaned and oiled the guns. One evening in the spring, seven of us were together. We were in a happy mood. Someone told a story of how Joe Roche, my uncle's man, and three other old-timers met at the Cross. They adjourned to a pub for a while and came out feeling much better. The martial spirit asserted itself. They even felt numerically stronger. They decided that at least they should drill and march through the town. Joe was appointed instructor.

'Fall in!' said Joe.

He drilled and dressed his men, first in single file and line, then two deep. And then to the delight of the boys at the corner, Joe shouted: 'Form fours! It must be done, be damned, boys, although there are only three of ye there,' he added.

Here someone suggested that we go through a little drill, as a token for a new start. Six of us were drilled by my brother Pat. So the start was made. After that evening men were coming in one by one, until the Company's strength reached its old level. In a few secluded spots we met and drilled.

One fine Sunday evening four of us left my uncle's house and strolled along the road to the village. My uncle, Joe Roche, Tadhg Buckley and myself comprised the party. We met a neighbour on his way home from the Cross and sat down on top of Achan Riach while talking to him. He told us the news and casually asked us if we were going to Ballyvourney to the play. We knew nothing about it and asked him what the play was and who the players were. The play he said was *Handy Andy* and the players the Macroom Dramatic Company.

'*Handy Andy*,' said my uncle. 'It is hard to teach an enslaved people. Isn't it remarkable how the shoneen is not happy until he is trying to belittle the people of Ireland and show them to the world as a race of uncouth and ignorant savages? Pearse and his comrades are not dead a year and these so-and-sos from Macroom must come and resurrect the Stage Irishman again. Come on lads, we will go to Ballyvourney.'

My uncle's dog was with us. We liked his company but we decided his presence might complicate matters for us later. We left him at the cottage of Johnny Curley, a friend of ours whose son was a Volunteer. As I was leaving the cottage, I saw a stirabout stick.

'Johnny,' I said, 'will you give me a loan of that stick?'

'I will and *fáilte*,' said Johnny, 'but I'll give you a nice walking stick if you like.'

'No, Johnny, thanks,' I said, 'this is quite good enough for the Stage Irishman.'

Johnny blinked his eyes and I knew he did not understand, but I had not time to explain.

Near the Cross we met Mikeen, Tadhg Buckley's brother.

A hard man who had long ago been drummed out of the British Army. A splendid cavalryman, but all the King's men could not bring him to discipline. He would take a horse when he wanted one and suffer for it later. Their varied punishments failing, they let him go.

He was never a Volunteer, but was always ready to help and in later days often risked his life to warn us of the enemy. Now he eyed us as if he knew we were on some business bent.

'We are going to Ballyvourney, Mike, to see that play,' said my uncle with a roguish smile.

'I was thinking of going there myself, but I must tell some of the boys,' said Mike.

We knew the 'boys'. They were all about Mike's own calibre. No harm in them really. They would go to a wedding as strawboys, or stand at the village cross at night, until all hours, singing songs. Indeed one of the four of us now going northwards to Ballyvourney had been one of their company, Joe Roche.

We reached Ballyvourney in good time. In the main street outside the hotel stood a motor car. Enquiries confirmed that the players had come and were refreshing at the bar for the play. We sought out a few locals whom we knew. They got busy with us talking about the play among the crowd that was gathering in front of the hall. Soon some hundreds had assembled. Each new disciple spread the light. The people had not understood. Soon the disciples were in the majority.

A lamp blazed in front of the hall. Two RIC men were on duty. We kept out of their sight, well back in the crowd. We had no desire to enlighten them of our little organisation. People were still coming, and each of us held a position to intercept them. To the right of the entrance door and just in the shadow I saw Mikeen with a dozen of his 'boys'. They appeared to be in a pensive mood, like real connoisseurs of the drama.

The players had entered the hall a long time since. It was already past the hour advertised for the start of the play. Then someone announced from the entrance door that all was ready. A placard had told us already that the admission fee was one shilling for front seats and sixpence for the rear. No one stirred in the crowd. The RIC got uneasy. They moved about as if trying to fathom the mystery. I would have given a good deal to see both the body of the hall and the stage at the time. One of Mikeen's men came to my side.

'I have a bad sixpence here,' he said, 'and I'll never again get the opportunity of spending it. Would it be all right to go in? I'll find out what's happening inside.'

'Go ahead,' I said.

He got in all right. Indeed I think he need not have spent the bad sixpence. Afterwards he told us of the financial side.

'Six-and-six they got,' he said, 'and that included my good money.'

Presently a spokesman appeared on the doorstep. He made an appeal to the good taste of the people of Bally-vourney. They had come to show them first-class drama, indeed they should be glad to have this opportunity …

The hall was made entirely of iron. The first rock falling on the roof sounded like the crack of doom. It was the first of an avalanche. The front door was closed. The RIC approached Mikeen's men. The men retired into the shadows. The law then infiltrated into the 'masses' in front. The bombardment continued.

Suddenly the door opened and out rushed a big man. With the bluster of a bully he challenged the best man in Ballyvourney to fight him. No one moved, but some laughed. I recognised him as one of those who had offered to defend the barracks in Macroom on the night of my uncle's arrest. I groped on the ground for some missile. I was so tightly restricted by the crowd that I could find nothing. He retired again behind the closed door. It was then I realised too late that I held a stick in my right hand. I promised myself that I would not forget again.

The RIC now endeavoured to clear the crowd from the front. They started moving them slowly down the lane. A civilian appeared from nowhere helping them to push individuals here and there. I concluded that he must be one of the players coming again to the assistance of the RIC. I waited. Presently he approached, pushing people near me. The RIC had stopped, but he continued energetically. I reached my right arm across a couple of my neighbours and the stirabout stick rapped sharply on his head. The RIC made an industrious movement forward, but saw only a small ripple in the crowd as I disappeared. The bombardment continued and soon the garrison surrendered. As they came out the crowd voiced its disapproval. The RIC shepherded them practically unscathed through the 'masses', save for a few shrewd cuffs and 'toes' hastily administered. They sought the solace of their hotel.

The four of us repaired to the other hotel, where we had tea. We sat by the fire talking to a group of friends for some time, then we started on our homeward walk. It was a fine, calm, frosty night. We had nearly reached Poul na Bró, about a mile from Ballyvourney, when we heard a car behind us. Hastily assembling some dumps of ammunition in the dykes at both sides of the road, we waited. They came, and as their lights fell on us, they gave a defiant yell at the country yokels who did not appreciate their genius. A *feu-de-joie* rattling on their enamel warned them that they were still in hostile territory. With increasing speed they vanished from our sight.

We stopped on Poul na Bró bridge, over the River Sullane, while Dan Harrington lit his pipe. By the light of the match I could see his face. It wore a happy smile. He spoke. 'Well, be damned boys, *Handy Andy* could hardly be described as a huge success you know.'

4

1917 – A NOCTURNAL EXPEDITION

The efforts to obtain armaments of any kind at this period were truly remarkable. Money to buy them could be obtained somehow, but there was no market which sold them. Very small quantities, and small material only, could be smuggled in from abroad. The arms in the hands of the enemy provided the only source of supply. Our own authorities prohibited us and kept prohibiting us from trying to capture these. This prohibition would last for a long time yet. We were therefore invited to make our own war material.

We already knew how to make slugs, or buckshot, for shotgun cartridges. We possessed, or made, small machines for loading and capping cartridges. We could even make the powder for them. But the bombs and grenades which we were directed to make proved to be entirely a waste of time.

We set to work to make them in all shapes and sizes.

From then on a housewife had no worry about the disposal of empty treacle tins – they disappeared. Neither had the farmer any broken or unsightly pig troughs to encumber his haggard. Cast-iron pots, with any suggestion of a crack, were helped by the hammer to their final dissolution. A like fate overtook the ancient kettle.

This was our method of grenade making: a layer of viscous concrete was first poured into the tin. Then followed a judicious arrangement of scrap. Another layer of concrete. Then more scrap. And so on. A wooden core, to provide space for the explosive, and the tin was put aside to set. When required, the explosive was inserted with its detonator and a suitable length of fuse.

Having made a large number of these things, we were anxious to test them. The testing ground was a field next to my uncle's house. We arranged targets standing around, to intercept the shrapnel. From the fence we threw our grenades, and then stooped in its shelter. After each explosion we inspected the targets. We tried all our types of grenade and bomb. My uncle had been a keen observer at the tests.

'Well, Dan, what do you think of them?' asked someone.

'Well be damned, they may have some moral effect,' he answered.

Another waste of time and energy was the manufacture of the shotgun bayonet. We got a pattern, complete with clip, and were directed to make some dozens. We made them. They never did any harm to the enemy, but they nearly killed some of us who were engaged in their manufacture. Some day soon they will be found at the bottom of a bog-hole and will be classified by archaeologists as: *Spears, Early Iron, Offset Socket.*

At this time, we had not a single service rifle in our Company. Neither had we pistols nor revolvers. One evening my brother Pat, returning from Cork city, brought with him two new .38 revolvers. Unanimously, one was presented to my uncle, while my brother, now our Company captain, got the other. My uncle must have correctly interpreted my thoughts as I examined his revolver, for he directed me to erect a target and we had a few shots. A short time afterwards I met him on the road. He put his hand in his coat pocket and drew forth a .45 police revolver, which he handed to me. If, instead, he had handed me the riches of the world, they would not have been more welcome. It seems he had helped a neighbour in some way and this man, whom we all knew but never suspected of keeping a gun, went home without a word and returned with this fine weapon. He well knew what would most please my uncle.

One fine evening in early summer, the Company was assembled by special notice. The time was late, about half-past nine, and the place of assembly was Den Buckley's barn loft, in the village. Two oil-gas lamps gave us light. Presently our captain entered, accompanied by a stranger.

The newcomer was evidently a city man. My brother called us to attention and introduced him. He was an organiser from Brigade HQ. First he spoke in Irish, then continued in English. Having dealt generally with routine work, drilling, etc., he concentrated on armaments. When the address assumed the character of a lecture, my brother directed us to fall out and be seated. We made ourselves comfortable on bags of grain along the wall and some, seating themselves on the floor, reclined luxuriously against the sides of the bags. Thus fortified, we listened.

Our lecturer dwelt at length on the importance of acquiring arms. This irritated my uncle, who was patient only up to a certain point. He interrupted to state that damn well we all realised that, and that having tried all sources, we had come to the conclusion that the only way to get them was to take them from the enemy. Permission to take them was all we wanted. The lecturer explained that he himself had no say in the granting of such permission. In the meantime, every effort should be made to augment our supplies of shotgun ammunition. Cartridges should be loaded with slugs and, of course, to make slugs, lead was necessary. Lead should be acquired by any and every means. Here there were hardly suppressed smiles as the lecturer's eyes ranged along the class. The ways and means for providing lead in our district were indeed varied and unscrupulous if judged by peacetime standards. Peace reigned in the land according to our oppressors, or ought to reign according to the supporters of our oppressors. These partisans we made pay a heavy toll. Unwillingly they supplied us with lead, even from the roof valley-gutters of their unoccupied mansions.

The lecture continued, with the emphasis on the lead. At last my uncle again interrupted to remark that we had an abundance of lead, that with us it was a redundant commodity, while every other material was in short supply. The lecturer retaliated by saying: 'You could *not* have enough lead.'

Here my uncle smiled, as his great sense of humour asserted itself. 'We have plenty of it,' he repeated, and after a pause he added in an undertone: 'We have a reserve supply as well.'

The lecturer heard all and eagerly asked: 'A reserve supply, where is it?'

Here we craned our necks to study more carefully the expressions on both men's faces. We guessed my uncle had something in mind which would make us laugh at any rate. He feigned reluctance to answer, then at length said: 'Ah well, it is in safe keeping.'

Then came the query: 'In safe keeping! What kind of people are minding it?'

'Oh, quite inoffensive people,' answered my uncle.

'Who are they?'

'The rude forefathers of the hamlet,' was the reply.

A roar of laughter followed. Most of the Volunteers

knew or guessed what he meant. Gray's *Elegy* some had read in their schoolbooks, while others had heard my uncle recite it. Others, who never heard of Gray, knew where the reserve was located. Not so the lecturer. Certainly he had heard of Gray, and knew the *Elegy*, but could not associate it with a dump of lead.

'I don't see the joke,' he said.

'Well, I'll tell you,' said my uncle. 'Over in the churchyard is a tomb with lead coffins in it. That is the reserve I was referring to.'

'I see,' said our lecturer, and paused for a while. He spoke again. 'I think you ought to get that lead,' he said.

'I would not think so at all,' said my uncle, and added: 'We do not want it at present, and very likely may never want it. In the meantime, it is safer where it is. Where could you get a safer hiding place for anything? Besides, we have no ambition to emulate Jerry Cruncher, the body-snatcher in the *Tale of Two Cities*, until it is absolutely necessary.'

'I always heard,' said the lecturer, 'that country people were very superstitious, and afraid of ghosts and fairies.'

My uncle laughed. 'There are not many in this room,' he said, 'who would baulk at going at midnight to the church-yard, and even at visiting the old Captain.'

The 'old Captain' was one of those of the landlord class who rested in the vault. Indeed, it was known as 'the Captain's Tomb'.

'But,' my uncle added, 'it is neither fear of ghosts nor fairies, or superstition which keeps us away, but respect for the dead.'

The lecturer made no further comment. He walked to the door and, opening it, looked out at the night.

'It is a fine night with a full moon,' he said. He turned back to the room and, looking straight at my uncle, said meaningly, 'There is no time like the present.'

It was a challenge to Dan. Dan got to his feet, and said, 'It is indeed the witching hour. Get a few tools, lads, a spade or two and a shovel. I suppose we would want a bar or a pick also, and yes, be damned, a sledge.'

Most of the tools were found in the car-house underneath the meeting room. Soon seven of us were on our way to the churchyard at the other end of the village. The rest of the Company had been sent home, but, before going, had nearly all volunteered to stay and help.

As it was so late there were no lights in the houses as we passed through the village. The moon shone with full brilliance. We passed silently through the small side gate of the graveyard and were soon among the shadows cast by the 'rugged elms'. We easily found the tomb. The moonlight shone directly on it. It was a large structure with high iron railings on top. Someone put the question: 'How do we get in?'

An answer came: 'Through or over the railings.'

My uncle spoke: 'I would not say so. I have some recollection of hearing old people talking about a burial here. I got the impression that the entrance was outside the vault altogether, that you dug out here somewhere and went down a stairway and entered underneath the ground level.'

'Old Pad would know about that,' someone ventured. Pad's son Tadhg was with us. He was sent with a companion to get old Pad out of bed to show us where to dig.

This evoked a protest from our organiser. It was a pity, he said, to disturb an old man and bring him out of bed at that hour.

'Yeh, not at all,' said all the others. 'He is a hardy old lad and as sound as a rock.'

The morale of our visitor appeared to be getting a little frayed. Indeed we had noticed, when the project had passed the discussion stage, that he appeared to regret his over-enthusiastic sponsorship. However, it was now too late.

Pad presently appeared between his two custodians. His silvery beard and patriarchal mien were in themselves awe-inspiring. The place, the time, the moonlight, the nature of the venture, did not help to dispel that feeling. My uncle greeted Pad, then in a few words explained what we required. Pad nodded gravely, walked slowly to one side of the vault, and, starting from the middle point of that side, walked away from it at a right angle. About eighteen feet from the wall he stopped and pointed to the ground.

'Dig there,' he said.

'Take Pad home lads,' said my uncle.

Immediately work was started. Scarcely had the first blow from a pick broken the silence, when our visitor spoke.

'That will do lads,' he said. 'I thought ye would never venture it. I owe ye an apology.'

My uncle spoke up. 'We will see it through now then,' he said.

A noise from the far end of the graveyard focused our attention. Something was moving there. It seemed to be coming nearer without making any further noise. Sometimes it disappeared only to reappear again. At length it resolved itself into the figure of a man, a tall man, a military-looking man. Sure enough, a man in uniform. The moon shone on some metal object above his face. A cap badge. Slowly he came, now concealed by the elm trunks, now revealed. Now he was quite near. His buttons shone. 'The Captain!' someone whispered. Now we could see his face.

'Halt there!' I heard near me.

It was my brother who spoke. A revolver gleamed in his hand. It was levelled at the intruder. My uncle held another levelled gun. The figure coming on so surely, stopped.

'Oh, for mercy's sake, lads!' he cried out.

We laughed with relief. It was not the Captain. It proved to be a friend of ours, who kept a shop in the village. Coming home late, he had met one of the Volunteers who told him of the expedition. Thinking that he would frighten the expeditionary force by appearing as the ghost of the Captain, he had donned an old military tunic and cap, and had followed. As he was crossing the graveyard wall, remote from us, he was tripped by a briar and fell heavily. That was the noise we had heard.

'Had I known,' said he, 'that ye carried guns, I would now be in bed.'

The interruption proved to be the end of the adventure. Our organiser made a fresh appeal and this time succeeded. We repaired the small damage done to the greensward and retired. It was now very late and, of course, we went to bed.

The following day, my brother, my uncle, the brigade officer and I met again.

'Dan,' said our visitor, 'was it to show me that ye were not afraid of ghosts that you insisted on carrying on with last night's job?'

'No,' answered Dan, 'but I was thinking of our lack of money. With it we could manage to buy a few guns now and again.'

'How would last night's job enrich us?' asked our guest.

'Well, I'll tell you,' said Dan. 'Those old fellows in that tomb were very rich, and liked to carry the world's goods as far as they possibly could with them. The devil a fear but they have at least a lot of jewellery in there ...' Here Dan winked at Pat and myself.

'Dan,' I said, 'would you take the rings off a dead man's finger!'

'I'd pull them off his old nose, be damned,' he replied.

5

THE MOUTH
OF THE GLEN

Sunday, the eighth day of July 1918, was a fine day and a historic one for Ireland. For the first deliberate and armed attack on enemy forces since 1916 was carried out on that date. It was a small but completely successful operation and this is how it happened.

Johnny Lynch was captain of D Company, Ballingeary district. He left his house at Béal a' Ghleanna to travel the winding downhill road to Ballingeary, about three miles distant. With him was his wife. Behind them at home was their four-month-old son Dinny. Their objective was second Mass at half-past eleven.

For the first two miles of their journey they went over the road trodden by O'Sullivan Beare and his people, three hundred and fifteen years before. They passed by his first camp at Acharus, and by Poul na Circe, where he lost his horse, An Chearc. Johnny and his wife would have been glad to meet Donal and his mighty warriors. But, alas, what were they fated to meet instead? A grey horse and sidecar, the driver on the box-seat, and two armed RIC men, one on each side. Each had a carbine between his knees, a spiked helmet on his head, a sling of ammunition across his shoulder and a baton hanging from his waist-belt. In each tunic pocket was a notebook. This would be used whenever the disaffected, to HM King George V, used only his tongue. As the horse slowly climbed the slope to historic Acharus, the police may have ruminated thus:

'Ah well, O'Sullivan Beare passed on through the glen, well over three hundred years ago. Good job, too. Troublesome fellow he was, by all our records. Not much doing since he left. Of course, there was that Céimaneigh business, and a fair share of moonlighting, anything to keep the ball rolling. And that 1916 outbreak lately. The government made a good job of that. Of course, those Volunteers are drilling again. But they have no arms. Who are these down the road? Lynch and his wife. That fellow is no great *iontaoibh*, as those Irish speakers say. They are going to second Mass now.'

'The Peelers are going to Ballyvourney,' said Johnny to his wife. 'The *aeriocht* at Coolea has been proclaimed, and this is the contribution from the barracks below.'

Johnny's keen eye had noted the Lee-Metford carbines,

but his further thoughts were forestalled by his wife's remark: 'I'd like to see those fellows come back empty-handed.'

Johnny made no comment, as he was working out the details.

On the way to Mass they met Tadhg Twomey, bound for Coolea. Johnny instructed him to get one or two Volunteers, on his way or at the *aeriocht*, and to be at his own house at the glen in good time to intercept the police on their return. Johnny met Liam Twomey, Tadhg's brother, in the village. Liam readily volunteered to take part.

In the meantime a large crowd of people were assembling at Coolea, about five miles north of the glen. Strong forces of military and police were converging on Coolea also. The Volunteers were watching their movements and instructing the people accordingly. Finally the military and police took up positions in and around Coolea, while the people all moved further west into the mountains of Cúm Uí Chlumháin. There an enjoyable *aeriocht* was held, while Volunteer scouts watched the enemy. I was watching a young Scotsman in kilts who stood on a height playing the war pipes. His name was Ian MacKenzie Kennedy. He was staying at Túirín Dubh, the home of Liam and Tadhg Twomey, and years later, during the Civil War, gave his life for the Irish Republic. As I watched him, my brother Pat came to me and asked me to give a revolver to Dan T. MacSweeney. He told me that Dan, Jamie Moynihan and Neilus Reilly were going to Béal a' Ghleanna with Tadhg Twomey. I volunteered to go too, but he answered that it was full-grown strong men who were wanted there, as they were to grapple with the police. I was disappointed but had to put up with it.

There were six men assembled at Johnny's house in good time. Three were from the Coolea and Ballyvourney side – north of the road; three from the Ballingeary side – south of the road. A seventh man, Jer Shea, from the village of Ballingeary, had already been sent to the highest part of the hill to watch for the coming of the police. There were now more men than were necessary and Johnny suggested that three should make an effort to intercept the two RIC from Inchigeela barracks, who would probably return by Derrinaonig. The others opposed this, as there was the possibility that the police from Inchigeela might also select the glen as their homeward route. Johnny was overruled. It was a pity.

At that early period it was imperative that, having decided to do a job of this kind, the utmost precautions should be taken to conceal the identities of the participants. British law still functioned perfectly, nay, it was now doubled-edged. The RIC were still the eyes of the enemy. Johnny therefore produced some burnt corks and each man blackened his face. Each man wore a mask, made from a handkerchief, with holes for his eyes. Two carried small .38 revolvers. Johnny carried his shotgun, with two cartridges loaded and primed by himself. It was impossible to buy cartridges at the time.

Béal a' Ghleanna was four hundred yards distant from Johnny's house. There were perpendicular rocks on the northern side and on the southern side the glen fell steeply away from the road, which here and there had been built up from a depth of fifty feet below. At one point a little plateau, unprotected by a wall and lower than the road level, jutted out over the glen. Here were stationed Dan T. Mac-Sweeney, Liam Twomey and Neilus Reilly, lying concealed amongst the heather. The job of Dan and Liam was to deal with the policeman facing south, peacefully if possible. Directly across the road from them and behind a pillar of rock, Johnny, Tadhg and Jamie waited. They had not long to wait.

Their plan was complete. Johnny was to step out on the road and present his shotgun. Jamie and Neilus were to seize the horse, cut him away from the car and let him go his way. They were then to take the sidecar and throw it over into the glen. This would help to discourage people from driving the RIC.

They saw the grey horse a long way off. He came slowly up the straight from Renanirree. He disappeared around the first bend. He would not reappear until within a few yards of them. They could hear his hoofbeats and the echo of his hoofbeats. Now they could hear voices. Presently they could make out a few words. 'Machine-gun' was one. It was repeated, and then Johnny's ear caught one complete sentence. He knew the policeman's voice that uttered it. He was a bad lad and what he said confirmed that fact: 'They (the people) did not run until they saw the machine-gun.'

Just then Johnny stepped out on the road, his shotgun levelled. With his towering figure and masked and blackened visage, he must have appeared a most menacing apparition. The driver thought so anyway, for he left the box-seat with so much precipitation and maintained such an acceleration, that the onlookers thought he would leave the ground and fly. He did leave the ground, too, for meeting the wall of the glen, he dived over it and was lost to sight.

Johnny paid scant attention to the vanishing driver. He concentrated on the policeman on his side of the car. He saw him snatch, with finger and thumb, at the magazine cut-off. Then Johnny knew that the breech wanted a cartridge. Swiftly laying his gun on the ground, he reached upwards and, grasping his opponent's tunic, dragged him off his seat. The RIC man reached the ground on the flat of his back, still clutching his rifle with both hands. Johnny now transferred both hands to the rifle and a struggle for possession started. As he had reached upwards for a hold on the tunic, the policeman snatched at his mask. He had torn it off, and had brought a bit of skin from Johnny's nose as well. That was a serious matter, as he might now be recognised. Besides, the mark on his nose would persist. Johnny had little doubt about the outcome of the struggle; it would be hard to meet his equal for physique and spirit. As the policeman reached the ground a revolver had cracked at the other side.

Dan and Liam had jumped from the heather simultaneously with the others. They had a longer distance to travel and had to scramble a little to get up on the road. They presented their revolvers. Their opponent reached for his rifle, which lay on the seat inside him. As he grasped it a bullet scarred his neck deeply. He fell from his seat and lay bleeding on the road. Jamie and Neilus worked quickly, too quickly as it transpired afterwards. Cutting away the horse from the sidecar, they caught the shafts and, driving the car over a bank, released it. When it came to rest at the foot of the precipice it was a sorry sight.

Johnny's opponent still clung to his rifle. He shouted for mercy and said he was a married man with a wife and family depending on him; yet he would not relinquish the rifle. Johnny, for a reasonable time, had taken him as easily as he possibly could. He had risked his life and liberty to spare him, even after hearing him boast of how the machine-gun had frightened the people at Coolea. Now he had to treat him roughly, and when Johnny straightened himself up holding the captured rifle, the RIC man lay on the ground bruised and vanquished.

'Where is the other rifle?' someone asked.

Jamie and Neilus had assumed that it had fallen on the

road with the wounded policeman. Actually it had remained on the seat of the car and was now gone down the glen with it. Johnny and Liam climbed down. They found it undamaged. It had fallen out on the thick heather, early in the sidecar's wild career. The booty was now checked and found correct. It comprised two magazine Lee-Metford carbines, two slings of .303 with fifty rounds in each, two belts with batons, two spiked helmets (for the overawing of simple people) and two notebooks.

The whole party went up the hill on the north side of the road. Here the Ballyvourney men and Tadhg Twomey had dumped their bicycles. Tadhg took his and, making a detour by Gougane Barra, came home to the village of Ballingeary. Jamie, Neilus and Dan also cycled home around the mountain road. Johnny and Liam dumped the helmets, batons and other useless stuff in a nearby *béilic* – a jutting rock under which the sheep slept at night, and often many a good man as well. With the carbines and ammunition they again came down to the scene of the ambush. The police had gone. Crossing the road, they skirted by Johnny's house. Here, in a grove, they found Jer Shea's bicycle. Evidently Jer had gone home across country and intended to return for the bicycle that night. Liam had his bicycle also, and both were in the wrong place in case of an early morning search by crown forces, which was now a certainty. They had already decided that, when darkness fell, they would take the rifles and ammunition away to the south, across the main road from Ballingeary through Céimaneigh to the west. This would eliminate all risk of their being found in a minute local search. They now decided to take the bicycles also.

Meanwhile, what of the police? Evidently they roused themselves up and caught the horse, which had been grazing along the dykes of the road. The wounded man mounted the animal and his comrade led it by the head. Thus they made progress down by Acharus, not indeed as dignified as that of the morning. They met Mick Callaghan. With unfeigned surprise he asked: 'Yerra what happened ye at all, at all?'

Under the circumstances one could hardly expect a civil answer. Compared with their polished, well-equipped and martial bearing of the forenoon, they now looked a total loss.

'Ah, someone will pay for this,' was the reply he got from Johnny's opponent.

The man scarred by the bullet said nothing. Indeed, it was a matter of regret with the Volunteers who knew him and especially with Johnny, who had experience of his courtesy during a raid on his house, that he should have been hurt. They rejoiced when they learned that his wound was not serious. His name was Butler. There was scant sympathy for the other man's bruises. His name was Bennett.

'Ní raibh órlach na máille d'á chorp na raibh rian cic air.'

That was how an old man in the village described his condition. On the previous evening this truculent policeman had cleaned his rifle outside the gate of the barracks. With this accomplished to his satisfaction, he had proceeded to display his skill. Catching the weapon by the barrel, he had spun it in the air and again caught it as it fell. This he did repeatedly for the delectation of the simple peasantry. Well, he had had his fling. So had the RIC as a body. The people were tired of them and their overbearing, strutting tyranny. The 'Law' and the 'Force'. Yes, and the Crowbar and the Battering Ram. The Torch and the Buckshot. The Bayonet and the Bullet and the Baton. These tools had been always associated with the 'Law'. The 'Force' was the eyes and the ears and the power behind the 'Law'. This is how my mother taught me the English alphabet:

A for the Army that covers the ground,
B for the Buckshot we're getting all round,
C for the Crowbar of cruel ill-fame,
D for Davitt, a right glorious name. (etc.)

In the favouring dusk, Johnny and Liam, the slings over their shoulders and the carbines tied on their bicycles, rode down the road towards Ballingeary. At Cathair Cross they left the road and, taking the bicycles on their shoulders, crossed over Carraig na Dabhaire, down through Gurteen Owen wood,

up Coom Dorcha, down Doire na Buairce, out on the road
at Scrahán Mór, near Muing na Biorraí, where Smith was
buried after Cath Céimaneigh. Down Túirín Lahárd, across
the river at Túirín Dubh, and out on the road to Céimaneigh.
Along the road to Céimaneigh for a short distance, then up
the steep boreen to Richie Walsh's. If they had come stagger-
ing under the weight of bags of gold for Richie, they could not
have been more welcome. Apart from the events of the day,
before they left the road at Cathair Cross, the cross-country
march, with bicycles and rifles on their shoulders, was a feat
that few could accomplish in the daytime. The width of the
roads they crossed was the only horizontal and smooth surface they met. Even the bed of the river they crossed was
rough. The little fields they met all sloped at a steep angle,
and the stone fences were often ten feet high, on one side
at least. Rocks, stones of all shapes and sizes, with furze and
stunted black and whitethorn in between the stones, covered
the ground they travelled. They were giants who did it.

After tea and a talk with Richie, they filled bags with
straw and climbing further up the rugged hill to a *béilic* they
knew, made their bed and slept the sleep of the just, not
far from 'Lua's fairy lake', where Michael Doheny had also
rested. Poor Doheny's thoughts could hardly have induced
pleasant dreams, since he had seen dismal defeat, while
Johnny and Liam had at least tasted victory.

6

A QUIET PERIOD

Except for the periods of actual military activity, the ordinary Volunteer attended to his everyday duties in private life. This was not an easy matter, at any time, especially for the man who had to do a hard day's work. To work hard, or indeed to work at all, it is essential to have regular sleep and rest. Youth and enthusiasm replaced sleep and rest during many of these years of preparation and conflict. The fire of youth burned brightly in most of us. But I remember, above all, the few who had to depend on enthusiasm alone to sustain them. One of these, a small man past middle age, joined the Volunteers on the very first day of their inauguration. He had worked for a farmer for a few shillings a day since his early youth. Now, with over half a hard life behind him, he cheerfully took up the additional task of working for his country by night, without hope of remuneration, but with the certainty of shortening, and the chance of losing, his life. His name was Neilus O'Connell, but he was known to us by his *nom de guerre,* Louth. During his long service for Ireland he saw many a day breaking. It was his greatest pleasure. May he enjoy the brightness of an eternal dawn.

In the autumn of 1917 the time had come for me to leave home and go to a secondary school. I viewed the prospect with dismay, as Volunteer reorganisation was in full swing. One of my sisters, a secondary teacher, stepped into the breach and saved me. She taught a younger sister and myself and prepared us for the Junior Grade examination. We had a most enjoyable school year, and I had plenty of time for Volunteer work. But good times come to an end and June 1918 came quickly. We passed our examination and were free from study for the summer months. The attack on the RIC at Béal a' Ghleanna early in July and a little subsequent martial law activity brought on the autumn again. The Conscription Bill, passed on 16 April 1918, had caused a scare amongst people opposed to, or not interested in, the cause of Irish independence. It had caused a good deal of amusement amongst the rank and file of the Volunteers, and had provided extra work for their officers, who had to deal with a large influx of recruits while the scare lasted. But it was merely a temporary hosting, like that of King Wire's donkeys.

King Wire was an expert manufacturer of wire goods, muzzles, strainers and the like, who attended every horse fair in the south of Ireland. While he walked through the throng of people and horses, he worked unceasingly with hands and pliers on the roll of wire slung over one shoulder. When his feet stopped he bought donkeys. Thus while his eyes surveyed his prospective purchase and his tongue got busy to bargain with a fine humour, his hands never rested. No donkey on the market went home unsold. All went into his carelessly kept herd.

One evening in Macroom I remarked to him: 'You have a big stock today, King.'

'Most of those will have departed by morning,' he replied.

Early in September 1918 I left home for Rockwell College in County Tipperary. On the evening before I left, I handed over my revolver and ammunition to my comrade, Louth, who promised to keep them safely for me. I felt, I believe, more lonely than the average youth going to a boarding school for the first time. I had heard and read and seen a little of our country's long struggle for freedom, and longed for the day when I could take a man's part in it. I knew that that day could not now be very distant. In the meantime, during the quiet period, I would submit to the bondage of learning. It might also be described as a political period. Sinn Féin had already taken three seats in by-elections from the Irish Party, which attended the British Parliament at Westminster. It was an indication of coming events. It showed how weary the people had grown of sending representatives to make futile speeches on the 'floor of the House'. For practical purposes, they might as well have been engaged at sweeping the floor.

In the atmosphere of Rockwell I soon discovered a strong national spirit and a great love for the Irish language. It prevailed alike amongst the college authorities, the teaching staff and the students. There was even a link with the Fenians, in one old lay brother. He was very old, but his spirit was still young. Up to the last he was still the unrepentant Fenian. In December 1918 he insisted on walking some miles to record his vote in the General Election. It was a vote against the parliamentarians and for his own comrades, the Fenians or Volunteers, and he made that very clear. The results of the General Election emphasised the same condition, for Sinn Féin swept the board and only a few 'floor of the House men' were left. I was at home for the Christmas holidays when the results became known.

I was glad to get home, since I had heard of the ravages of the influenza which had swept over Europe after the Great War. It had killed a few of the Volunteers in our district. The Volunteers and Cumann na mBan had helped the people immensely. Where an entire household became ill, or were otherwise handicapped, units from each organisation took over the duties of nursing, heating and food supply until the family was on its feet again. Their fearless and efficient assistance won the hearts of people hitherto bitterly opposed to them. Undoubtedly they saved many lives and, where necessary, they helped to coffin and bury the dead.

I heard the tale of disaster with regret, since all the victims were my neighbours and comrades. To cheer me up, other contemporary incidents were related.

During the epidemic many remedies and medicines were tested and suggested. Whether or not it was suggested by the medical profession, or at a meeting of shareholders, I cannot tell, but whiskey proved, if not an effective, at least a popular and palatable medicine. Nor have I any evidence to show that even a single dealer, licensed or otherwise, audibly expressed the opinion that it was worthless. Rather have I authority of rumour that at least one publican, entirely devoted to the health and welfare of the general public, evolved a laborious scientific process to ensure that each and every member of his increasing clientele would have at least some small percentage of his life-saving *aqua vitae*. On this particular evening, a group of Volunteers and neighbours on their way home from a funeral stopped outside his premises. They were tired and weary from want of sleep. They decided to try some tonic to keep up their spirits.

One of the neighbours spoke to the Volunteers. 'I know ye do not take strong drink, lads, but by all accounts the whiskey here will do ye no harm.'

All entered the pub and stood alongside the bar. Soon it transpired that there was no other drink in the house but whiskey. After a little discussion, everyone, teetotallers and all, decided to sample the elixir.

Standing at the bar, midway in the line of men, was a

Volunteer whose Christian name was Éamon. He had already tasted whiskey, a few times, just enough to know what it should taste like. Having once discovered the characteristics of anything, there was little danger that he would keep the knowledge to himself. In other words, he was very outspoken. The publican busied himself with spigot and measure, and soon a row of glasses was ranged along the bar. An oldish man of the neighbours took his glass and raising it said, 'Sláinte!'

Every man grasped his drink and repeated, 'Sláinte!'

All, excepting Éamon, tasted it and lowered their glasses at once. Eyes were cautiously turned right or left, and then slowly left or right. Most of the Volunteers looked puzzled and they tasted again. They had expected that at least it would make them cough. The older men regarded each other, some with a sorrowful look, some with a grim smile. It was their unspoken verdict. But what would Éamon's verdict be? Would he accuse the publican directly of putting water in the whiskey?

A loud exclamation focused all eyes on Éamon. He also had tasted.

'Dammit! … Dammit,' he said again as he placed his glass sharply on the bar, 'who put the whiskey in the water?'

So saying, he turned and walked out the door. Smothering laughter as best they could, all hurriedly replaced their glasses on the counter and followed suit. In the open they gave vent to their feelings. It was some time since they had indulged in a hearty laugh. Now they had the opportunity. The weakest stuff they had ever tasted, *aqua pura* almost, had proved a better tonic than the most potent.

The holidays over, I returned to Rockwell. Here, so far, we had seen no sign of the influenza. Within a fortnight it had a firm grip on the place. It was milder than the earlier form of the epidemic, but it caused the death of one student. With a few others, I managed to keep on my feet and we were allowed home. It was near the beginning of March when we were recalled again. Since we had lost a good deal of time we were granted no Easter holidays and we worked on to examination time at the beginning of June. Meanwhile, events of great political importance had happened.

The greatest event was the assembling of the First Dáil Éireann or Irish Parliament on 21 January 1919. Sinn Féin had contested the General Election on an abstention from Westminster policy and a guarantee to set up our own assembly. The people had given them authority to set up that parliament. It was now legally accomplished, but yet it was only a gesture, a finger pointing along a certain road. It could not function while an alien parliament with its powerful force behind it still functioned. That force must first be neutralised. The Volunteers had already undertaken that task, against foreign and native opposition. Now their own parliament directed them to proceed with the good work. Henceforth, the Volunteers would be known as the Irish Republican Army.

In Rockwell I had been kept well informed of the trend of events in the outside world. On the night before we left for home, after the June examinations, a concert was held in the refectory. It was attended by the entire personnel of the college, directors, teaching staff and students. It gives me the greatest pleasure to think of that night, now half a lifetime distant. The stern dean of studies, and the dean of discipline, who hid a great love for the boys behind impassive features, now came down and mingled with us for a few joyful hours. There was no formality. One of the Fathers would call on a student to sing, while the students in turn would call on a Father to favour them with a song, which he invariably did. I remember that all the songs sung, whether Irish or Anglo-Irish, had in them the resurgent spirit of that time. All too soon the hours passed and the last songs were sung. The last was the 'Battle Hymn' composed by the Countess Markievicz for the Citizen Army, and sung by a student, Willie Jones.

Armed for the battle, kneel we before Thee.
Bless Thou our Banners, God of the brave!
Ireland is living! shout we exultant;
Ireland is waking, hands grasp the sword.
Who fights for Ireland, God guide his blows home;

Who dies for Ireland, God give him peace!
Knowing our cause just, march we triumphant,
Living or dying, Ireland to free!

The second last was sung by Father Michael Maher. It was
'Limerick is Beautiful', a patriotic song composed by a Limerick man, Michael Scanlan. As is usual, Ireland is depicted as
a beautiful woman.

Oh, she I love is beautiful, and world-wide is her fame,
She dwells down by the rushing tide and Eire is her name.
And dearer than my very life, her glances are to me,
The light that guides my weary soul across life's stormy sea.

I loved her in my boyhood, and now in manhood's bloom,
The vision of my life is still to dry thy tears aroon;
I'd sing into the tomb, or dance beneath the gallow's tree,
To see her and her hills once more, proud, passionate and free!

Although I was leaving for home early next morning I felt
lonely as the concert ended. I knew that I was seeing that
good company for the last time. Yet I can always see a clear
image of it and hear again those manly voices.

At home again, I found among the people and the Volunteers an increasing enthusiasm for learning the art of war.
War material and weapons were very scarce. It was now

accepted that the only available remedy was to acquire them from the enemy. There were three RIC barracks in our area, Ballyvourney, Ballingeary and Inchigeela. Preparations for a simultaneous attack on the three were now begun. The time was favourable since the quiet period still continued. The battalion officers met weekly at a disused farmhouse in the parish of Kilnamartyra, the most central point of the area. The same old house was ideal in every way as a meeting place for guerrillas. It was set in a lonely little glen among the rocky hills. It could not be detected from any point of the compass, not even from the air, yet it occupied a commanding position and one sentry could watch over every approach to it. We used it for a munition factory as well as for a meeting place.

On the evening following my return from Rockwell, Louth and my brother Pat invited me to a meeting at the old spot. I gladly accepted. The three-mile walk in the dusk, the prospect of meeting my comrades and the anticipation of a talk by the turf fire in the old kitchen enchanted me. As we set off, Louth handed me my revolver and ammunition.

'You will find a few cartridges missing,' he said.

'Oh, what matter, Louth, you could have used a few more,' I replied.

My brother laughed. 'His opponent thought that he had used quite enough,' he said.

'What! Louth,' I exclaimed, 'have you become an exponent of the duello? Who was the gentleman? Had he blue blood in his veins and all that. Surely it was an affair of honour?'

Louth laughed.

'The time and place were all right,' he said. 'It was just after daybreak on the bank of the Sullane. My opponent might be described as a gentleman of leisure since he does nothing but saunter along the banks of the river. He might have the blood of kings in his veins for all I know, but he is a water bailiff this long time. As for the affair of honour, it was forced on us. Your brother and I were coming home late one night or early in the morning. A few of the Macroom lads were with us. When the sun rose we decided to have a look around Línn na Mullach to see if we could come by a salmon. The bailiff opened fire on us from cover. We drove him from his cover and tried to catch him, but he got away from us. The Macroom men caught him at home the same day and relieved him of his gun. He must now have recourse to the sword,' he added dryly.

At the meeting I met Donncadh MacNeilus for the first time. He had come to our area since he was much wanted by the British. He had worked in Cork city as an engineer and had been an active Volunteer. One morning the RIC came to arrest him. They almost surprised him in bed, but he resisted fiercely. He used an automatic pistol, wounding a head constable. The weapon jammed and he was overpowered and taken to Cork county gaol. The Cork Volunteers effected his rescue in a brilliant daylight coup on 11 November 1918. Since then he had moved about the western half of the brigade area, fully armed, and was now staying with us. He was welcome, for his splendid personal qualities as well as for his capabilities as an engineer. During the remainder of the summer and until late autumn, I was to see much of him.

The barrack attacks were to take place on a date in September and he was busy with us on the details of preparation. The RIC had, at this period, a special technique of patrol, which they practised in the daytime. Four of them would leave a barracks, sometimes by the back door, and go across country on foot. They carried only revolvers. Evidently their authorities calculated that such a number with rifles would invite attention and fall an easy prey to a local IRA group. Sometimes the patrol used bicycles. Either way, they were a menace to a man who moved about alone.

One afternoon in the autumn I went to meet MacNeilus at a certain house about four miles from home. It was accessible by a quiet byroad, so I took a bicycle. I carried my revolver inside my coat. As I neared the house I rode down a steep hill at a fast rate. Near the foot of the hill the road made a double turn. Rounding the first bend, I ran into the RIC patrol of four, with bicycles. They had dismounted and were pushing their bikes uphill. Two came first, one on either side of the narrow road. Twenty yards behind and similarly disposed came the other two. I rushed between both pairs and around the second bend. I believe they hardly saw me. Within a few minutes I was at the house and in the kitchen.

The good woman of the house greeted me and pushed me before her into the parlour. There, the man of the house, his son and MacNeilus were seated at a table, calmly drinking tea.

'Did ye see those police?' was my answer to their greeting.

'We did,' they replied. 'They were here.'

As I sat at tea with them, they told me of a very near clash. A few minutes before, they had been seated in exactly the same positions. The RIC patrols had been the subject of discussion.

'Traitors they are,' said the man of the house, 'prowling about the country, dragooning the people like the old yeomen did. They should be shot at every door.'

Just then his wife entered the room. 'There are two police in the kitchen,' she said, 'and two more outside.' So saying she returned to the kitchen quickly.

In all the old farmhouses, because of the big open hearth and chimney, a corridor called the 'entry' connected the parlour and kitchen. As our hostess returned to the kitchen, the sergeant of the police stood just inside the kitchen door. He could see into the parlour, but could not see the table.

Nevertheless, it was plain that he suspected from her hurried movements to and from that room that she had given warning to some party. Meanwhile, the other policeman had moved further into the kitchen.

At the warning, MacNeilus had quickly arisen, a long Parabellum in his right hand. Remembering that that gun had not a cartridge in its breech, he swiftly drew the hinged bolt with his left hand and let it home again with a crash. That sinister sound smote on the sergeant's ear with telling effect. He turned pale and for a few seconds stood motionless. Then, turning, he walked out of the kitchen, followed by his comrade. Quickly the four reached the end of the short boreen, recovered their bicycles and rode away. They left in good time, as Donncadh, with a .45 revolver to supplement the pistol, was edging forward to attack. That sergeant appeared to have been gifted with no small share of common sense.

Our programme for September was cancelled by GHQ. While they commended us for our enterprise, they advised that it was better to wait until other areas were ready for a more widespread operation.

7

INCHIGEELA

We started the new year, 1920, badly. It is said that first attempts are always the worst, and certainly our first effort at the capture of a barracks was a lamentable one. The sympathetic youth of today who question me about 'battles long ago' say feelingly: 'Ah, ye had very poor equipment compared with that of the enemy, and ye also lacked men.'

Well, on the night of 2 January 1920, our equipment was indeed poor, but quite good enough for the work in hand. Neither was it lack of men that caused the failure. The fact of the matter was that it was due to a surplus of indifferent men.

Up to that time the numerical strength of the Volunteers had increased to a peak point. True, it had been higher because of the conscription menace to the youth generally, but, that scare having passed, it had dropped again. Yet it needed a little taste of war to separate the chaff from the grain and to reduce further mere numbers to a fighting unit of quality. In plain words we had, up to that very night, been carrying a lot of 'passengers'. Here I must say that credit is due to every man or woman who did his or her best and went as far along the road as they were able. Some cannot endure what others can, nevertheless they must be honoured for having tried and failed. I always reserved my contempt for the jackeens who held aloof and never helped in any way. But I had the pleasure also of meeting young men who never joined the Volunteers, but who, in an emergency, came forward and gave us valuable assistance. They were indeed the unknown warriors.

My uncle's house at Knocksaharing was the rendezvous for the men of Kilnamartyra and Ballyvourney that night. The old thatched house had often before been a meeting place, for Fenians as well as the IRA. Our objective was the Inchigeela RIC Barracks. Our men had all turned up well before the appointed time and had been directed to go on to a further point near the Macroom–Inchigeela road. My uncle, a local Volunteer and I were told to wait on for half-an-hour and then follow. That half-hour was considerably shortened by Dan's humorous stories and comments. First he picked up his shotgun and, having looked through the barrels, tested all its action.

'Dammit, Mick,' he said, 'try that front trigger spring.'

I tried it and found it broken.

'Could you fix it?' he asked.

'I could,' I answered, 'but not now. The only thing I can do now is a makeshift job.'

Finding a piece of elastic cord, I tied the trigger forward to the trigger guard.

'It works all right,' he said, 'but do you know what, we have damn bad tools to fight an empire with.'

Then musingly, while he regarded the old gun, he quoted: '"Some one of us three, Herminius, shall ne'er again see Rome." No matter,' he added brightly, 'have a look abroad, Mick, and see what of the night.'

I went to the door and looked out.

'The moon is rising, Dan, and there's snow on the ground,' I reported.

'Well, well,' he said, ''twill be like the battle of Hohen-linden. I knew a bloody scut of a shopkeeper one time and he had the first verse of Hohenlinden printed on a card in his shop window.

'On Linden when the sun was low,
All bloodless lay the untrodden snow,
And dark as winter was the flow,
Of Iser rolling rapidly.

'Underneath the verse was a parody on it, praising the quality of his rotten tea. I bought a pound of it and it nearly poisoned me. Next time I was in town I went into his shop and quoted for him a parody I had made in the meantime:

'But thievish X— where e'er he go,
The public shall the robber know,
And lower still the price shall go,
Of tea that's rotting rapidly.'

It was time for us to go. Taking our guns, we went outside. Dan locked the door and, stooping, placed the key in a crevice of the old wall. It is remarkable how a small action is still fresh in the memory after the passage of years, while a major event is hardly remembered. The little incident impressed itself on my youthful mind. The man of fifty-five, leaving his comfortable house and excellent farm on a night of snow. Behind him his good fire and his books, his greatest pleasure. Before him the rude elements of mid-winter and the wrath of an empire whose reactions would be ruder still. He had already had ample experience of that rudeness. His offensive weapon now was a dilapidated fowling-piece and his allies a few badly armed youths.

We went down the moonlit meadow, along the edge of a small bog and climbed out on the Lios Buí road at Judy's Gully. Keeping the road, we passed southwards to Ahacunna and crossed the Toon road and river at Doire Airgid bridge. That lovely road led upwards through the rocks and groves of Doire Airgid, through Cluan Siar and Cooleen of the hazel glens, until it brought us out on the main Macroom–Inchigeela road at Ros Mór. Near here we met the others who had preceded us and we all moved on to Carraigacurra. Here some were directed to cross the Lee and go westwards by the fields until they reached positions immediately across the road from the barracks. With these went my uncle and I. The others went on to the village to meet some men from Ballingeary and to close in from the north and west. Groups were detached to block roads and hold the barricades against enemy interference.

The barracks, a detached building, stood on the roadside, facing east. It overlooked a field across the road from it. We came from the southern side of that field and passed by the front of the barracks, sheltered by the road fence. With two others, I was allotted a position in a gateway, with a slanting view of the front of the barracks. My uncle was nearer the barracks, behind the road fence. We had got into our places silently and no one was the wiser. It had been impressed on every man engaged in the actual encircling movement that no one was to make a move which would betray our presence to the enemy. It had previously been noticed that most of the police visited pubs and other houses, and there was a great chance of finding the barracks door open and only one or two of the garrison inside, unprepared. This was the case when we arrived. A local scout brought three Volunteers by the route we had taken. One of them saw a policeman in front of the barracks and quite close to him. What did he do? Fired two shots at him and, to make matters worse, missed him altogether. The RIC man, of course, dashed for the door, which was wide open, and shut it behind him. Two Volunteers, one my uncle, who saw him run, fired hurriedly in an effort to stop him. They had little chance of hitting him, since they were taken by surprise, the distance was short to the doorway and the light none too good.

Those two first shots closed the door, in more senses than one, against an easy victory. The RIC man had only come out to take the air. Had he been let alone he might have strolled up the village street. In that case, we could easily have grabbed him and pulled him in to our gateway, without raising any alarm. Had he remained loitering around the barracks gate, any two men, ostensibly on their way home, could have seized him. A few more, with revolvers, through the open doorway, would almost certainly find inside men who were totally unprepared. Now they were settled down behind their loop-holed steel shutters and were busy with rifles and small hand grenades. Two of their comrades were in houses in the village when the firing started. One of them, Constable Tobin, tried to get back to barracks, but he was shot down. He later recovered from rather serious wounds caused by shotgun slugs. The other hid himself and was not found.

A useless and prolonged exchange of fire was maintained

by some of our men with the barracks garrison. The police bombs exploded with great violence quite near some of the Volunteers. At length a humorist amongst them remarked, 'Those things must be all empty.'

This evoked a hearty laugh, which the sergeant of the police must have heard, for he shouted, 'Fire away, lads, glass is cheap,' to show that his own morale was sound.

In vain we waited for news from a party of picked men who had been sent to breach one of the gables. Later we learned that, just as they had started to work with a will to break down the wall, some Volunteer had come and shouted an order to them to retire by the way they had come. This they had reluctantly obeyed and when the officer in charge, who had gone on a circuit of the barracks, returned, they had gone. Mystified, he with others started a search for the party. They had taken the tools with them and by the time they were located it was rather late in the morning. Undoubtedly there were alternative methods to the breaching of the gable, and had that failure been foreseen, others, like petrol bombs through the roof, could have been quickly substituted. It was my first acquaintance with Conny Creedon, a merchant in the village. He came out to the middle of the village street to offer us four or five barrels of paraffin he had in stock.

We returned home sadder, but certainly much wiser men. We had gained nothing from the enemy but a little experience, which would prove useful to us. In future we would not put our trust in numbers, but rather in quality. The following day we learned of the capture of Carrigtwohill barracks. With no better tool than a wall brad, the men at the gable had made a small hole in the wall. Inserting some gelignite, they had blasted a large breach in it. Through the breach a small party entered and the police surrendered.

We were not to get again the opportunity we lost that night. The police took steps to strengthen their defensive positions, and the lesson of Carrigtwohill was not lost on them. High up in the windowless gable, they broke out a small loophole for dropping bombs. This they lightly plastered over again. From the gable outwards they threw a heavy entanglement of barbed wire. They also reinforced the garrison.

I doubt not, if the matter had been left in the hands of our own local battalion, that we would have regained our lost ground. But now the brigade took a hand and told us to sit up and learn a lesson. Young as we were, we were yet anxious to improve our education. Some of us had indeed made certain suggestions for the overcoming of the new difficulties. We were told to watch our elders working and profit thereby. We humbly acquiesced and waited for the demonstration.

On the night of 7 March we had again encircled Inchigeela RIC Barracks. I stood with a storming party drawn up at the edge of the barbed wire. Three officers from the brigade were busy with a trestle of guncotton. While they inserted the primers and detonators with the fuses, I wondered with others how they were to cross the wire. Provision had been made (on paper) to block the bombing loophole. Another trestle stood by to effect this. But the wire had yet to be crossed. Very soon all was ready. The taller trestle stood like a Roman standard over our heads. I looked higher up to see the kites, but it was too dark. The 'brass hats' moved to the edge of the wire and stopped. Now was our time to learn something of the science of tactics. But we were to learn nothing. Very quietly we were withdrawn again. Ourselves alone knew of our discomfiture. The kites went home hungry.

We came home in a very bad humour. The following day, as if to add insult to injury, the RIC sergeant of the barracks at Ballyvourney cycled alone to Renanirree, about halfway between Ballyvourney and Inchigeela. Jamie Moynihan of Gortnascarthy and Dan Sullivan, his neighbour, had been with us at Inchigeela. They got the news that the sergeant had passed up the hill at Ráth about a mile away. Taking shotguns with them they waited at the foot of Ráth for his return. The same official, whose name was Flynn, had, from an early date, been very active against the rising tide of opposition to the old order. He took a particular delight in the destruction of the tricolour when it was displayed in his area. He had a specially made torch mounted on a long staff for the purpose and he always carried out the operation himself. At length, however, Con Seán Jer cured him of his incendiary tendencies.

Con hung a tricolour on the telephone wires at the village cross of Ballyvourney. The sergeant had already burned down several from the same setting. Had he looked closely he might have noticed a fold or wrinkle in the middle or white band of his latest target. Evidently he had noticed nothing, for he applied his torch. Within the fold was a white paper, which wrapped half a stick of gelignite complete with detonator and a very short bit of fuse. He watched with evident satisfaction the flame climb upwards towards the green. Already the white was more than half eaten. Suddenly he found himself seated on the road as if a giant had pushed him backwards. The flag had disappeared with a loud explosion. Thoughtfully he arose and went home. The next day he passed by the Cross again. A new flag flew from the old staff. He did not bring his torch to burn it. He let it wave in triumph until it wore away.

Now he was coming at a smart rate down Ráth hill. Two men with guns called on him to pull up. He tried to get through. A shot aimed low knocked him off his bicycle and wounded him slightly in the leg. Jamie and Dan searched him. A notebook he carried contained the information he had got from a local informer about Jamie's own movements and the movements of others. Soon after this incident the names of both Jamie and Dan appeared in the *Hue and Cry*. It made no difference. At one time it would have been of importance to the wanted men, who, in order to escape arrest would have had to leave the country. Now it did not matter as we were all on active service.

8

BALLINGEARY BARRACKS

Whitsunday, Domhnach Cingcíse, was always a big day in Ballyvourney and will be so forever, if fourteen centuries be taken as an indication of established custom. The day is not the feast of Saint Gobnait, but is a second day set apart in each year to do her honour. Starting on the eve of Whitsun, a stream of patrons visit her shrine to pray. Some keep vigil there all through the night. The many crutches abandoned there give striking proof that prayers to Saint Gobnait are effective. Having visited the shrine and prayed, the people come down to the village to refresh and enjoy themselves. I am not going to pretend that the primary object of this great influx of people to Ballyvourney is always solely to honour Saint Gobnait by prayer alone. Certainly it is the aim of many of them. But the young people and children seek amusement as well. And who can blame them? The sound of their merry laughter and the sight of their happy faces must be appreciated as much in heaven as on earth. Old people become young again as they watch the young enjoy themselves. The passage of half-a-century is ignored, and once again they are children who have come to the Cingcís for the day.

It was Whit-Saturday night in 1920. My brother Pat and I had come to Ballyvourney and were strolling along the village street. We met Jer Carthy. Jer was a Volunteer from Ballingeary, our intelligence officer for that district, and a good man he was. We drew aside to a quiet spot and Jer gave us the news. For some time past he had been closely watching the movements of the RIC and Black and Tans in Ballingeary. The RIC had recently been reinforced by Black and Tans, and their combined strength was now fourteen men. They all lived together in the RIC barracks in the middle of the village, across the street from Shorten's public house.

The road proper between the barracks and the pub was not a very wide one. Three cars abreast would fill it. The barracks was an ordinary two-storey house with a door in the middle. About fifteen feet in front of the building a wall ran along the edge of the roadway. It was breached by a small gateway straight opposite the front door. The wall was about three feet high. On a fine sunny day it would be an inviting and not uncomfortable seat for an active and leisurely young man. Seated on it, his legs dangling, he would have a close view of everyone who passed by on the highway, or passed through the doorway of the pub across the road. The pub, like the barracks, stood back from the roadway, but had no wall or other obstruction in front. Like the poles of a magnet, one building attracted while the other repelled.

Jer had noticed how, for the past three or four Sundays since the weather had got fine, a number of the Black and Tans regularly sat on the wall after lunch. The number varied, but on one occasion as many as ten were there together. At least seven or eight had always come out. What did we think of it? Very few of them had ever come out armed. They sat on the wall talking and joking and commenting on the people who passed them by. They did not appear to be anticipating any attack, in the daylight at any rate. The only caution they displayed was that they did not go far afield from their barracks.

We decided to get in touch with all the Volunteers who possessed revolvers. These weapons were very scarce at the time, as were all other types of firearm. Before midnight we had mustered twelve men. Of these only four carried service revolvers. Six were armed with smaller bore guns, while two could almost truthfully be said to be unarmed with miserable pocket revolvers. Little planning was necessary. To get into Shorten's pub without attracting the attention of the enemy across the road was the first and most vital part of the operation. It should also have been the easiest. Yet it was that which thwarted our scheme.

We settled on reaching Ballingeary village at about a quarter to two on Whitsunday. We left Ballyvourney just after noon, cycling away in twos and threes. People were still coming towards the place while we were going away from it. That in itself was not a good start, but would do no harm, since there was no means of quick communication between the two places at that time, and the people we met would mind their own business. We cycled southward over the bridge of the Sullane, and, turning east, we wound around the base of the Curragh hill to Cathair Ceárnach (the Fort of the Champion) in the valley of the Dubh-Glaise, the Dark Stream. Our road led us upstream and westward for a mile along the only placid stretch of the Dubh-Glaise, until we reached Átha Bhuadh, the Ford of Victory. On either side of us the little green fields showed bravely on the steep slopes they had conquered from the Curragh and Rahoona hills. In front of us rose Gort Uí Rathaille, its foothills covered with stunted oak, birch, hazel and holly. Above us, in a clear sky, the noonday sun of May shone brightly. Within us were the thoughts of youth, stimulated by the legendary associations of our surroundings – Cathair Ceárnach of ancient victories and Átha Bhuadh which, according to local tradition, will one day be the scene of our ultimate triumph.

Crossing Átha Bhuadh by the little bridge, we were soon

climbing the steep and wooded slope of Gort-an-Imill. Reaching the top, we paused to regain our breath and to view a most unusual and beautiful extent of rugged scenery. Mounting, we cycled down into Renanirree, on the road from Macroom to Béal a' Ghleanna and Ballingeary. Three further miles of a stiff uniform climb on the bicycles brought us to Béal a' Ghleanna. Here we rested and discussed the final arrangements for our project. When we mounted again it would be all a downhill three-mile run to the village of Ballingeary and, barring accidents, a non-stop one.

But now a serious question was raised, a question which should, there and then, have put a stop to our visit for that day. We had, we all admitted reluctantly, picked out the worst possible day in the year for the job. Why the devil had we not thought of that last night? Most of the young people of Ballingeary and district had just passed by the barracks on their way north to Ballyvourney. So had people from places as far distant as Bantry. The enemy had just seen the last of them pass an hour ago. The RIC knew well where they were heading for. The village would be almost deserted. Then twelve young men on bicycles would come from the north. Had they come some four or five hours later, they would doubtless pass as a party returning home after the day.

We then discussed the value of making a detour and coming into the village from the west. It would look all right just now about midday, we decided, but afterwards we should wait at Shorten's for two hours or more before the time for action. It would do no good now at any rate.

What then was to be done? Postpone the job until next Sunday, go back to the Cingcís at Ballyvourney and enjoy ourselves for the evening? What do ye say to that? Would it not be the wise thing to do? Of course it would, but every time we had been over-wise we had gained nothing.

Soon we were mounted and speeding down the winding road. Turning right when we met the main Macroom–Bantry road, we crossed the bridge parallel to the gable of the barracks and fifty yards distant from it. Turning left and in single file, we ran down the short incline and pulled up in front of Ben Shorten's public house. Leaning our bicycles against its long front wall, we entered. There was no sign of life around the barracks across the way and, despite the warm day, the bar was deserted. Presently Ben himself appeared. We gave him greeting and while some ordered soft drinks, others of us scanned the windows of the barracks from the depths of the shadows of the bar room. For a quarter of an hour we saw nothing. Then a Black and Tan strolled out to the gate.

From the moment he had appeared at the doorway he became the object of an intensive study. He carried no arms and appeared wholly at his ease. He bore all the appearance of a person who had just had a good lunch and had walked aimlessly out to idle in the sunshine. He was bareheaded, a

WHERE MOUNTAINY MEN HAVE SOWN

big man, young and not ill-looking. Sauntering to the gate, he stopped and stared straight in front of him into vacancy. Then his eyes ranged slowly up and down the road under his feet. Raising his head slightly his gaze appeared to become fascinated. We knew what interested him. It was our array of bicycles. He stiffened, rubbed his eyes, half turned, looked again and, completing the turn, walked quickly back and disappeared through the door of the barracks. Now, we said, the cat is out of the bag. We wondered what the result would be. It might be very favourable for us. If the Tans wanted to allay their thirst, they would doubtless cross the road to do so. Or if they wanted to satisfy their curiosity they might do likewise. We expected them to come and made preparations for their reception. Scarcely had the Black and Tan time to tell his comrades of the plague of bicycles, when we saw the reaction to his announcement. Faces peered cautiously from behind every window opening. We took good care that they would see nothing. We had instructed Ben to clear out immediately we would tell him of their coming. We had hoped that the more venturous among them would prevail, and that a strong party would dash across and enter the bar room through the wide opened door. After all, they were a poor-spirited lot. As the time wore on our contempt for them increased. We tried a number of tricks to draw them out. These were largely based on showing them that we were a harmless party, unarmed and out for amusement only.

Some sang songs, other went out in their shirt sleeves to look at their bicycles, leaving their coats and guns inside. It was no use. Finally Jer Carthy came up the street on a bicycle and came in. After a consultation with Jer, it was decided to try another ruse. We had now been two hours in the pub. We sent Jer away, after arranging to meet again.

After a lapse of a quarter of an hour, we left in a leisurely manner. Some talked loudly, while others walked a little unsteadily. We all laughed loudly and heartily at a few who were acting drunk. But no one of the twelve had touched any drink with a trace of alcohol in it. Getting hold of our bicycles, we started an argument as to which way we should go. All the time we were being keenly watched. Finally, we mounted in a disorderly manner and left in the Bantry direction, away from home. Rounding a few sharp bends of the road to the west, we reached the gate of Coláiste na Mumhan. Entering there, we hid our bicycles inside the hedge of the road and lay down on the grass. Very soon, Jer Carthy appeared again.

'Ye had not turned the second corner,' he said, 'when four of them came out and sat on the wall, but they have their revolvers with them this time.'

'We must only have patience, Jer,' said my brother, 'until more of them come out.'

Jer went off again. We sat or lay in the shade of the hedge and waited. Every quarter of an hour Jer returned and reported, 'There are three out now,' or, 'There are five out now,' and so on.

At length Pat said to him, 'When there are six out, Jer, come and we will have at them.'

Again Jer disappeared. Now started a very long period of waiting, whiled away by a thorough rehearsal of the procedure when we should return to the village. When the word came we were to grab our bicycles, each take the place allotted him in the file and take the last corner at top speed. Riding hard, we were to pull up on the raising of Pat's hand in front, lay down each bicycle swiftly on the road and get busy. The leading six would rush the door of the barracks, while the remainder would attack the men on the wall. It was a chancy business, but every man we had could be relied on to do his part. Each had eagerly intimated his desire to fight these Black and Tans under any conditions. Certainly, it was half the battle to have such men, and it would go far in countering the advantages possessed by the enemy in quality of arms and position. We waited on.

Suddenly Jer dashed in the gate on his bicycle.

'There are six on the wall,' he said.

The time had come. Quickly, but very smoothly, we got into line on the road and moved off without a hitch. Our pace increasing easily, we rounded the last corner at a high speed indeed. Soon we were rushing past the barracks. There was no one on the wall.

Pat threw out his left hand slightly and swung into Shorten's space again. Dismounting, he leaned his bike against the wall. We did likewise.

'We'll have another drink,' he said.

We disappeared inside the door. Again the innocuous drinks were ordered and again we settled down to watch. Again the faces appeared at the windows, watching for our next move. Another hour passed slowly. Two Black and Tans came out, wearing their holstered revolvers. They sat jauntily on the wall, their legs dangling. Whistling inanely, they kept time with their heels clicking together. They looked a low type. Possibly their comrades would be glad to get rid of them and had induced them to go out for that purpose.

It was now approaching six o'clock and our prospects were poor. As a last effort it was decided that the majority would act in a very drunken manner. Others, less drunk, would be doing their best to take them home. We hoped that others of the garrison might come out to enjoy the spectacle, or even try their hand at searching and questioning us. Dowd Cronin and I were to try first the effect on the two on the wall. We went through the doorway, Dowd protesting while I held his arm. He did his part well. He swayed to the middle of the road while he insisted that it was much too early to go home. I was the youngest member of the party and therefore it appeared reasonable to the audience that I should be quite sober. The Black and Tans on the wall were now laughing immoderately at Dowd's antics and at my difficulty in trying to get him to come home with me. I had succeeded in getting him to take hold of his bicycle. Both himself and the bike rocked perilously while one of the Black and Tans continued to laugh uproariously. Suddenly, the bike, which he held awkwardly by the near handlebar, leaned over too much and Dowd fell with it. He put out his hands, let the bike drop, and saved himself from a heavy fall by so doing. But the near pedal struck him sharply on the shins. It was a painful crack, and Dowd had a fiery nature and an explosive temper. The Black and Tan shouted with laughter. Dowd jumped to his feet in a fury.

'What are you laughing at, you bastard,' he said, looking at the happy warrior on the wall. 'I'll put you laughing at the other side of your mouth,' he added, his right hand reaching swiftly across his body and grasping his gun.

I threw my arms around him and wheeled him about to face the pub. The long, bright thirty-eight Smith and Wesson was out in his hand.

'Dowd,' I said, 'you'll ruin us!'

He slipped back the revolver. We could have managed the pair on the wall easily, and could even have taken their guns from them, but then we would have lost all our bicycles. For, had hostilities started thus, the fire from the barracks would, of course, have been directed on them. The wonder was that we did not lose them as things were, for the two Black and Tans made themselves scarce immediately. The door of the barracks was shut behind them and the steel shutters of the windows as well. Rifle muzzles appeared at loopholes. The others came out. Without undue haste, we took the bicycles and walked away with them. Stopping on the bridge, we leaned them against its northern wall. Then we stood along the southern side of it, facing the gable of the barracks and the rear portion of that building. Our arms folded, we rested on the parapet. We had some faint hope that the garrison, or some portion of it, might follow us as far as the bridge, even if only to verify that we had gone. In that case we would attack them at the bend and maybe take a few guns from them. It would be some compensation for a wearying day and enliven us on our journey home. But again we waited in vain.

We were about to turn away in disgust when a door facing us opened and the old RIC sergeant came out. His name was Appleby. A few years previously he had gained notoriety by arresting Claude Chevasse, a scholar, for speaking Irish to him. Claude Chevasse was brought before a bench of magistrates in Macroom and fined five pounds, a large sum in those days. I remember reading a parody in the *Leader* about the incident.

Oh, Paddy dear and did you hear the news that's going around,
Speak Irish to a policeman now, and you'll be fined five pound.

Sure the light of English learning soon our island will illume,
For it's fining Irish speakers are the J.P.s of Macroom.

I met with Sergeant Appleby and I took him by the hand,
And asked him if the Ballingeary folk the olden tongue had
    banned,
Ah, no, said he, they speak it still and fill my heart with gloom,
And fifteen miles away, alas, are the J.P.s of Macroom.

Now Applebys and grand J.P.s who dwell in this dear land,
Must put aside their upstart pride, and Irish understand,
We mean to strive and keep alive our tongue till crack of doom,
So to pot with all, both great and small, the J.P.s of Macroom.

Sergeant Appleby learned to mend his hand and later did
not give the enemy that information which would make
things difficult for the IRA. He definitely saved some local
men from the attentions of his own force, the RIC. He
continued on with the latter, but he took things as easy as
he could. Now he strolled about, his hands in his pockets,
his eyes on the ground. We watched for a while and then
someone coughed to attract his attention. He looked up
quickly and saw the long row of heads and shoulders above
him. Some of the old arrogance latent in him returned. He
squared his shoulders and fixed on us a stern and questioning look. Had he resumed his exercise we would have
walked away. But he did not. He maintained his posture and

his attitude indicated to us that we were quite long enough in the vicinity. But we were in no hurry.

'He'll read the Riot Act,' someone remarked.

My brother Pat spoke. 'Clear away out of that!' he said.

Sergeant Appleby shook himself indignantly. Imagine it! How the times had deteriorated! An officer of the Royal Irish Constabulary being ordered in to his own barracks by an unknown civilian, leaning at his ease on the village bridge, in the company, doubtless, of other disaffected persons! It was intolerable. But the civilian drew forth a long Webley revolver as if to second his demand. In a way that surprised us, Sergeant Appleby got inside that door and we heard a heavy bolt going home.

We mounted and turned left into the road to the glen. It was straight for the first three hundred yards. Scarcely had we covered one hundred yards when two RIC men on bicycles rounded the distant bend in front of us. In file, half of us took each side of the road. As they came near us we dismounted and closed in towards the middle of the road. They had to walk between our lines. We saw at once that they were unarmed. They wore only their bare, tight-fitting tunics. They had chanced a run out for the fresh air of the glen road, away from the barracks and the Black and Tans. They passed slowly through our lines, expecting every moment to be stopped. Our coats were opened and they could see our guns here and there, but no gun was drawn.

We had a certain amount of sympathy for them. Their faces wore a hunted look. Their own people had turned against them. They were trying to hold on to a job they did not like. We were hunted enough ourselves and weak enough, but our own people were on our side. That was the difference and I'm sure those two RIC men envied us. In any case, we would not be mean with them, and since they did not carry arms we would not subject them to the indignity of a search. No word was spoken and they passed through in silence.

Early in the afternoon of the following day, the Black and Tans brought Jer Carthy to the barracks. During their short time in the Gaeltacht they had learned the use of the suffix which denotes contempt. They now addressed Jer as Jereen:

'Jereen,' they said, 'you brought a crowd of murderers here yesterday to wipe us out.'

'They were not murderers, but friends of mine,' Jer replied boldly.

'You've a lot of friends, Jereen,' they observed.

'I have more friends than those,' was Jer's stolid reply.

'You're going to pay for yesterday's work,' they threatened.

'What happened yesterday? Were any of ye murdered?' asked Jer.

'No, but that's not your fault.'

'Why did ye not go out and pick up the murderers?'

'What do you take us for? A lot of mugs!'

'Well,' said Jer, 'if my friends are a lot of murderers, and if anything happens to me, where do ye fit in?'

There was a long silence. Then one of the Tans beckoned to the others and they all left the room, leaving Jer alone. Very soon one of them returned. He motioned Jer to follow him. They reached the hallway. The front door stood open. The Black and Tan spoke respectfully, 'You know the road home, Jer?'

'I believe I do,' said Jer, as he walked out, a free man.

Our visit to Ballingeary on Whitsunday 1920 might well be described as ill-timed and reckless. Had we met with Black and Tans of a tougher fibre, it is likely that they would have availed of one of the many favourable opportunities for attacking us. In such case we would have suffered heavily. But, as events proved, our opponents' morale was not high. Thirteen days later they were withdrawn from their barracks, which we immediately burned.

9

GEATA BÁN

It was the dusk of a summer's night in early July 1920. My brother Pat (our commandant), Neilus O'Connell (Louth), Patrick Cronin (Dowd) and I stood talking on the roadway at the Cross of Kilnamartyra. We talked, of course, of men and guns. We were just discussing the number of men, armed with shotguns, who were available in our local Company. A small but soldierly figure, wearing riding-breeches and putties, passed by with, 'Good night, lads.'

'Good night, Mick,' we replied.

It was Mick the Soldier, a brother of Louth's. He stopped at the corner out of earshot from us.

'There's a man who is anxious to join us,' said Dowd. 'He has had plenty experience of war, from 1914–1918. I think he should be a most useful man, since he is a crack rifle shot and is also a machine-gunner.'

Here Louth spoke. 'He is my brother, but I do not

approve of taking anyone who has been in the British service. However, please yourselves.'

Pat spoke. 'Some of our best men have been in the British Army, Neilus, and their training and experience have been of great value to us always. Didn't some of them join the British and other armies, just for the purpose of training themselves to be efficient soldiers to fight for their own country? Call over Mick, Dowd.'

Mick had been leaning listlessly, a lonely figure, his back to the wall at the corner. He had come home in 1919 from England where he had been demobilised. He had found a changed country. All the spirited youth worth knowing were, he found, in the Volunteers. He would not, could not, associate with the shoneen young men. He was a soldier born, nothing else, and these young men outside the IRA had not the martial fibre he wanted. Thus he had waited and watched with envy his brothers and old schoolmates go in the evenings to drill in some quiet place. Sometimes he had seen them at a distance at target practice with small bore rifles. He had longed to be with them, but felt that he was not wanted. True, they all greeted him cheerily, but never once hinted at the possibility of his joining them. His brother's attitude did not help either. Louth, after his day's work as a labourer, read Irish history often until far into the night. He could not understand how any Irishman could join the British Army. Well, Mick was not a student of Irish or any other history. When he joined the British Army there was no Irish Army to join. Besides, the politicians, then called Irish patriots, had urged the young men of Ireland to join the British Army to get Home Rule. Damn 'em anyway. He would ask Dowd to ask my brother Pat.

We saw Dowd reach him. We saw Mick the Soldier straighten himself with a galvanic start and come towards us as if walking on air. With precision he halted squarely in front of Pat and saluted formally. But his face was beaming with pleasure. He was about to join his own army.

'Well, Mick, you would like to join the IRA?' asked my brother.

'Oh, this long time, this long time,' was the reply.

'Would you be ready for action tomorrow morning, Mick?'

'I'm ready this minute,' was the reply.

So we chatted for a while with our new recruit, whose joy at being one with us was unconcealed and unlimited. Then we arranged a rendezvous for the morning.

The late morning saw six of us descending the northern side of Caherdaha hill. Terry, Louth's and Mick's brother, was the sixth. Mick carried a handsome, short Lee-Enfield service rifle, the only one we possessed. Pat, Dowd and I carried service revolvers, while Louth and Terry carried shotguns. By a quiet path we travelled in pairs to cross the Macroom–Renanirree road, and then a little plank bridge over the Sullane Beag. By hedges and along old boreens we reached the steps across the Sullane Mór at *Linn-Fia-Chait*. Here we met Jerry O'Sullivan (Jerry Conch). He carried a shotgun. We crossed the old steps and, winding upwards between furze-covered rocks, reached the main Macroom–Ballyvourney road at Geata Bán, not far from Coolavokig school. Here we met a section from B Company (Ballyvourney) and the two were combined to occupy fire positions on both sides of the road.

It would be hard to get a better natural situation for our purpose. Our aim was to halt and disarm the personnel of the first military lorry or two that came from Macroom. We wanted rifles badly and were determined to get them in this, the only way. It was not a common method at the time. Indeed, it was the first attempt in Ireland to capture rifles thus.

The spot selected was at the highest point of a long incline. This would naturally reduce the speed of the lorry or lorries, a very desirable factor from our point of view. A double bend of the road, between the firing positions, was a further advantage which nature gave us. An irregular rock rising from road level on either side completed an almost classically ideal ambush site. Around the bend, on high ground and remote from the approach direction, was stationed a heavy horse-cart, which could be run off the bank to drop in front of enemy transport and bring it to rest. The driver would here be covered by two marksmen with rifles, Mick the Soldier and Dannie Harrington of B Company. Theirs were the only two rifles we possessed. Across the road on the southern side, other expert shots were stationed, armed with shotguns, to shoot the driver if necessary. The remainder were disposed on either side so as to be in positions to deal with a second lorry, if two happened to come. Dowd and I occupied a niche or shelf in the face of the rock under the riflemen. Two signallers with flags were posted behind rocks, commanding the best views of the approach road.

As best we could we settled down to the weary process of waiting. Since the ground was favourable we were allowed to leave our positions and sit in a group to talk. This helped to pass the time with 'triumphant tales of recent fight and legends of our sires of old'. In the late afternoon there was still no sign of enemy activity on the road. We had eaten nothing since morning, and I doubt if many of us were provident enough at that time to bring a sandwich or even a piece of dry bread with us. At any rate, the unexpected happened. Up the approach road came a young lady carrying what appeared to be a white enamel bucket and a basket. Soon we recognised her. She was the daughter of the teachers of the school nearly half a mile down the road. She had the bucket full of tea, and the basket full of sandwiches. Apart from the renewed bodily vigour which the excellent food and drink gave, our spirits were raised immeasurably by the action of this young woman who had openly come to help, while others cowered and shrank away from us.

Of these latter I must speak a little. Very few people showed us any open hostility, but a very great number regarded us as a nuisance. It was hard to blame them. The hand of the British was still heavy upon them. On their fathers before them it had been much heavier. But the real 'bad old times' were gone, and the rackrenting and evictions. The teaching and work of Fintan Lalor and Michael Davitt had, by the Land League, effected this. The people owned their land. Now they had 'security' and they were content enough. True, in their hearts they would like to see the British gone, but who could put *them* out? Surely not a small group, here and there, of badly armed youths? Nothing could come of it but 'bad work', shootings and burnings.

Nothing came that day or the next. Then came 15 July. About 2 p.m. our group sat talking. My brother was with us.

'Watch the signal,' he said.

The signaller stepped down from the rock and, holding his flag low, shook it out. Then, raising it, he shot it forward. The flag flew off the staff and travelled a long way downhill. We burst out laughing. Now our signaller was in a fix. With commendable presence of mind he threw down the staff and raised both arms, his palms towards us. We readily understood. There were two lorries. The second signaller confirmed that on a nearer stretch of road. It was a long time before they appeared to us. They were coming very slowly. It was evident that they were heavy haulage lorries in a low gear for the incline. My brother studied them through powerful Zeiss field glasses.

'Pass the word,' he said. 'Let them through. They are laden with petrol and have only an escort of two on each lorry. We want rifles, not petrol.'

So they passed by, unconscious of the eyes that watched them.

About 3 p.m. one lorry was signalled. It was a Crossley, covered with canvas and well laden with troops. It came rapidly up the incline and on to the stage set for its reception. Had the fates decreed that the matter be left solely between the two contending parties, I think both would have been better satisfied. We would have got the arms we wanted, and the casualties amongst the occupants of the lorry would have been certainly fewer or probably nil. Now a car on the road, other than a military one, was, at that time, as rare as a four-leaved shamrock. However, there was one in Kerry and as the military Crossley came speeding uphill from the east to cross a certain line drawn by us across its path, the Kilgarvan Ford came from the west to straddle the same line at exactly the same time! The unexpected arrival of the Ford from the west gave pause to the throwing of the road block to allow it to pass. It passed and the pause was maintained until it was too late. Meanwhile, the Ford met the Crossley and, although going in the opposite direction, became its escort for more than halfway across the deadline to safety. Scarcely had the tails of both vehicles passed each other than a desperate effort was made by some to retrieve ill fortune. A furious fire was opened on the driver or in his direction. Mick the Soldier stood, his feet planted apart on the bare rock, while he poured rapid magazine fire downwards. Dannie Harrington stood a few yards from him to the west firing more slowly. Across the road, Con Seán Jer fired six shots from a double-barrelled shotgun, while near him, Jamie Moynihan rapidly worked another. A captain named Airey was killed beside the driver. The driver was twice hit, in the arm and neck. The lorry, out of control, hit the northern rock face a glancing blow, which tore off a spare wheel mounted on that side. Swerving across the road, it mounted a low wall which dropped inside to a depth of fifteen feet. It was touch and go for a good distance. If it toppled in, the survivors would have little fight left in them. But the driver tore it off the wall and straightened it for the road. He was a very worthy man and when we failed to stop him we wished him well. He drove off at a high speed.

Dannie had a few cartridges left in his magazine. Aiming carefully, he pierced the rear petrol tank. This gave us renewed hope. We set off in pursuit, running roughly parallel to the road. We had hoped to overtake it before it left the rocky country about Poul na Bró, where we could close with it again. We were doomed to disappointment. It had cleared the ground that would favour our approach and was stopped in the only patch of open country for miles around. Moreover, a party of soldiers from the Ballyvourney garrison had come out to meet it and had thrown out sentries. We approached as near as we possibly could without being seen. Having only two rifles, we could do no better than watch their movements and reflect with sorrow on our lack of proper arms. Had each of our men had a rifle, we could again have encircled the lot and driven them back on to the road.

As we watched, we saw a tall figure come slowly along the road from Ballyvourney. We knew him by his erect and dignified carriage. He was Master O'Brien, or Micheál Ó Briain as he preferred to be called, on his way home from school. The soldiers gathered around him, evidently questioning him, and gesticulating with their weapons. They were in an angry mood and we all knew that his life hung on a slender thread. Their captain had been killed and nearly every man in the lorry wounded. But they could not frighten Micheál Ó Briain. He was a gentle, saintly man, who would not harm any creature. He was also shy and retiring. But the heart within him was stout, and, while we trembled for his safety, I have no doubt Micheál did not quail.

Some of us asked my brother to allow the riflemen to

open fire on the soldiers and scatter them to cover. He told them to be ready to fire, but to wait for his word. He watched through the glasses for a long time, and once, when Micheál was evidently ordered back from the road to the southern fence, he again said, 'Be ready!'

Then Micheál sat down on the fence in a leisurely manner and our tension eased a little. Finally, they must have given him permission to go home, for unhurriedly he arose and unconquered he stalked away down his own rough boreen.

Many years before, when the 'Great House' flourished in Ballyvourney and when Irish nationality seemed dead everywhere, Micheál was at work in his school on a certain morning. Presently he noticed an undercurrent of disturbance in his classes. Investigating, he found that some of the children had pennies which they were proudly displaying to their less opulent neighbours. A little further research and he had the complete story of the fount of prosperity. As the children coming to school approached the 'Great House' they were met by a shooting party, travelling in open brakes or two-horse cars. These had thrown handfuls of pennies on to the roadway to see the children scramble for them. Micheál Ó Briain was shocked and grieved. There and then he delivered a lecture, and explained to the children that they belonged to a conquered race. They had been beaten by the sword, the torch, the rope, the pitchcap and other devilish methods of torture, and every effort by famine and deportation had been made to secure their final extinction. Yet, by the grace of God, they had managed to survive in the mountains and waste places. Their forefathers once had lived in the good land in the middle of Ireland. That land was now held by the English *bodachs* who had dispossessed them. It was some of these *bodachs* who that day had thrown the pennies to them. It was no shame to be conquered, but it was a shame to become a subject race. He expected them to show to the *bodachs* and to their own people that their spirit was not subdued and that as soon as possible they would rise again. He did not blame them for their action of the morning, but he expected them, now that they understood, to recover their lost prestige. The way to do that was to fling the pennies back to the *bodachs*.

The seeds the good man sowed that day fell on fertile ground. That evening, as the children were on their way home, they met the same shooting party. Again the pennies were thrown amongst them from the cars. The children again scrambled for them eagerly. But, to the consternation of the *bodachs*, the pennies were returned to them with a high velocity imparted by youthful arms.

10

TÚIRÍN DUBH AND CÉIMANEIGH

Túirín Dubh and Céimaneigh! It was not surprising that some event of note should happen in these places in our time. It merely repeated what had happened there before, for the spirit of Máire Bhuí lives on in her native Uíbh Laoghaire. Hers was no mere huckstering spirit that would recommend patience and politicians as a remote cure for Ireland's ills. The present was ever and always the time to deal with tyrants, she had declared. She did not want courts or other useless machinery for their trial, but a high gallows and a good rope. She counselled the young men to be always ready with serviceable pike and gun to meet the enemy. She exhorted them, over a hundred years ago, boldly to retake possession of the lands and homes of their ancestors. We understood how right she was.

On the evening of 27 July 1920, two heavy military

lorries passed through the village of Ballingeary. Their destination appeared to be Bantry, the nearest military barracks on the road to the west. They were laden with material for the maintenance of buildings. A large quantity of paint in tins added considerably to the weight of each lorry. They travelled about two hundred yards apart. Near the school at Céimaneigh, the soldiers on the first lorry noticed that the second was not in sight. They told the driver to pull in to the left and stop.

The old bog road, or *tóchar*, was never made to carry such a heavy vehicle with its solid tyres. An Irishman would have avoided the soft treacherous sides and kept to the road surface. But the foreign driver did not realise this danger. It transpired that the driver of the second lorry had pulled in to the side at Túirín Dubh even further than his colleague had done at Céimaneigh. Perhaps the solidity of the rocks around gave them a false idea of stability below their feet. In any case, both vehicles were now held firmly, with their inner wheels sunk to the axles. Their distance apart was roughly one mile.

The leading lorry had stopped in the shadow of the national school of Céimaneigh, which stood on a sharp height above the road. Nearby, and across the road, lived a local Volunteer, Dan O'Sullivan. Dan got his bicycle and left for the village of Ballingeary, to acquaint the Volunteers there of the chance that had presented itself. On his way he saw the position of the second lorry and noted the number of the escort. Between the two, the total personnel numbered thirteen. Eleven, a corporal and ten men, were armed with rifles, while the two drivers were unarmed. On arrival at the village, Dan sought for the brothers, Dannie and Jer Shea. He found them, and Dannie immediately left to mobilise some armed men in the shortest possible time. Christy Lucey and Liam Twomey were already near at hand in Túirín Dubh. Dan Lehane, Cahir, Pat Murray and Jack Moynihan were that day working at Doirín Flodaigh and, hearing the news, were quickly on the spot. Dan Thade Seáin (O'Leary), John Con (Cronin), John McCann (MacSweeney), Connie and Donncha Cronin and Jerome Creed all together made thirteen, the same number as the soldiers. The arms of the Volunteers, however, bore no relation in quality to those of their opponents. Eleven shotguns, a carbine and a nondescript rifle were the weapons. But the spirit makes up for the lack of material things.

The dispositions of the soldiers now made things a little difficult. Five riflemen guarded each lorry. As a connecting link between the two parties, the eleventh armed man patrolled the road. It was decided not to split forces for a simultaneous attack on both lorries and on the sentry. Instead, the plan was adopted of starting with a full strength attempt on the leading or Céimaneigh group. It certainly made matters far simpler than by the simultaneous movement of three parties, which would require fairly accurate timing and some system of signals and signallers. Besides, considering the poor quality of the arms, it was better to keep them all together to get the best effect. I do not know what a 'giniral' would have done with such a badly equipped party in such circumstances. Nothing at all probably, but even if he tried, he could not do better. The taking of each group separately had, of course, one serious disadvantage. Two of the three operations should be carried out quietly, otherwise the Túirín Dubh group might separate and take up unknown and perhaps impregnable positions.

Twilight comes early under the shadow of the hills around the Pass of Céimaneigh. As soon as the light began to fail, the full group of Volunteers began to move. Making a short detour towards the mouth of the Pass, they crossed to the southern side of the road. Keeping south and moving east, they soon came to the back of the school. Sending forward a scout to the schoolyard, they quickly followed on receipt of his signal. Stooping low, they were soon in line behind the front wall of the playground. In front and underneath them were the soldiers grouped near the lorry.

'Put up your hands,' a voice spoke quietly.

A little startled, the Tommies looked upwards. A long line of men, with guns pointing ominously, stood behind the wall. With little hesitation, the Tommies raised their hands. No noise had so far been made. The lads took the rifles and equipment and, leaving one armed Volunteer to keep an eye on the disarmed soldiers, departed. Keeping well out of sight of the road on the southern side of it, they moved eastwards towards Túirín Dubh. On the way they would deal with the sentry. Now this was not to be an easy job, since the road fences were low and in some places absent altogether. However, Dan Lehane and Tadhg Twomey took positions behind the pillars of a gateway about seven hundred yards from the school. As the sentry came abreast of them they rushed out at him. At first he backed away as if to get room to use his rifle. Dan followed him up, his shotgun inside the soldier's guard, and repeatedly asked for the surrender of the rifle. This at length the sentry did, by dropping the weapon, and the second phase was over.

The sentry was sent under escort to his comrades at the school.

Pushing on to Túirín Dubh, parallel to the road and south of it, the party soon halted not far from the second lorry. Creeping slowly forward in line, they came quite near the soldiers without being observed. It was now the twilight of this late July evening. As at Céimaneigh, the soldiers stood in a group near the lorry. The order to surrender was not in this case complied with. Throwing themselves flat, they took the best cover available around and under the lorry. A volley from the lads tore splinters from the woodwork over their heads and rattled on the ironwork. That helped them to decide otherwise. A white flag was raised on a rifle. The third and final phase of the operation was over. Eleven rifles and bayonets, with one hundred rounds for each rifle, was the prize of the day. No lives had been lost, not a man on either side had even been scratched. That was all to the good. The British government would regret the loss of the arms, but a Tommy or two killed or wounded would not worry them unduly. The arms would be used against them again, but they could get another Tommy for a shilling a day. Tommy did not look at it that way, however. He felt, and small blame to him, that his own life and limbs were of far greater importance to Thomas Atkins than was a rifle to John Bull. We looked at it in that light also and always, when Tommy was reasonable, gave him the benefit of the doubt. The Tommies from Céimaneigh were now brought over and the thirteen were taken to a nearby disused house. A fire was lighted, kettles were boiled and tea was made for them. After the tea, which they much appreciated, three men marched them, two deep, down the road through the village. Showing them the road to Macroom, they told them that they were free to go in that direction. They had not gone many miles when they met a strong relief party and returned with them to the scene of action. They found the two lorries completely burned out.

Having sent away the disarmed soldiers to the disused house, the lads now examined the lorries and their loads.

They found nothing of any military value among the stores carried. The large quantity of paint in tins appeared to be the most valuable material. Perhaps it might come in useful in the construction of dumps, mines and other things. In any case, they felt it would be wanton destruction to give it to the flames. Accordingly, they set to work and, taking it to nearby dykes and trenches away from the roadside, dumped it into them with little ceremony. But if they had been somewhat careless about the disposal of the paint there was, in the background, an unknown warrior who deprecated their rough and ready methods, and took steps to correct them. He belonged to that type which, in any emergency, hates to see wilful waste. A firm believer in suitable proverbs, he always did his best to realise them. The 'ill wind that blew somebody good' had often blown his way, for the simple reason that he had caused it to veer in that direction. Now he was making hay while the moon shone. Hardly had the Volunteers turned their backs, when this gentleman 'arose and twitched his mantle blue' and proceeded to transfer the paint 'to fresh woods and pastures new'. Working enthusiastically, he did not notice the passage of time or any undue activity in his neighbourhood. Not until he saw, by the light of a full moon, the glint of steel here and there around him did he take alarm. He made the mistake of trying to slip away through a meadow studded with cocks of hay. Some one of the soldiers of the relief party caught a glimpse of him and shouted tally-ho. Surrounding the meadow they started a diligent search of it. At length they located him under a cock of hay and dragged him out.

'Yerra lads,' he said ''tis I am glad to see ye. I was sure 'twas the other fellows were there.'

'What other fellows?' they inquired.

'The crowd that attacked the soldiers. I was with the soldiers all the evening helping them to release the lorries. When they were attacked I ran. The attackers followed me and fired after me. I hid under a cock of hay. I came out when I thought they had gone, and when ye came after me I hid again thinking they had come back.'

Strangely enough, they accepted the tale as a plausible story of his movements and released him.

11

THE SLIPPERY ROCK

It was half-past seven on the morning of 17 August 1920. Mick the Soldier and I were still in bed. Our bed was a good one, a mattress and a few blankets on the floor of Henry Browne's barn at Cools, Kilnamartyra. The weather was very fine, so fine that we had often slept in the open. One day, having slept the night before under the 'blue vault of heaven', someone complained of a headache.

'Ah,' said Joe Roche, 'that was the crack you gave your head on the rafter this morning.'

Someone tramped up the stairs outside our bedroom door and knocked. We admitted Seánín Donncha Eoin O'Sullivan, a Volunteer from B Company, Ballyvourney. We liked Seánín, and gave him cordial greeting. Then we asked him why he came so early.

'I'll tell ye then,' said Seánín. 'A cycle patrol passes from the military post at Ballyvourney through the village (Ballymakeera) to meet a convoy of lorries from Macroom.

The idea is to scout the road for the lorries. Then take up positions somewhere beyond Poul na Bró and wait until the lorries return from Ballyvourney. They number ten men and an officer with a revolver. They travel ten or twelve yards apart in single file. The lads are going to take up positions in the village, extended, like the soldiers, along the street, and rush out on them with sticks. They want a couple of revolvers to hold up the officer, and that's what brought me, to get a loan of two revolvers.'

I did not think much of the project: the time for such a job was past. My ex-soldier comrade thought less of it. Seánín did not fancy it either, but would do exactly as he was directed. I spoke.

'Well, Seánín,' I said, 'we will give you our revolvers now, but if you have no objection we will go with you since we are leisurely and we would like to see the fun in any case.'

'I have no objection,' said Seánín. 'I was told to bring two revolvers and if I turn up with two men armed with rifles and revolvers so much the better.'

Here I must explain that company areas were in reality parish or half-parish areas, and that between them there was a certain rivalry, the same rivalry that spurred the youth of one parish to excel in hurling or other games against the neighbouring parishes. The arms of the enemy were now the goal of all, but who would be the first to reach it?

Ballyvourney was four miles distant, due north. A road

led us straight down steep Caherdaha (Cathair Dáithí) across the little bridge at Átha Tiompáin over the Sullane Beag, up Ceann Droma, past Clohina, down Ceapach na Coille, by the foot of Rahoona hill, to cross the Sullane at Poul na Bró bridge, a hundred yards from the Macroom–Ballyvourney road. As we approached the bridge we noticed some activity along the far side of the main road. Men appeared to be lining a stretch of it. We wondered at this, as Seánín had told us that the village, nearly a mile to the west, would be the scene of the venture. We sent Seánín ahead to investigate. In a short time he returned with the news. As he approached we could easily tell that something amusing had happened. So it had.

The lads had, as they thought, unobtrusively occupied the eastern half of the village. Certainly, from the military point of view, it appears that they did it well. There were small, disused houses, sheds, laneways and corners that could fairly be described as no-man's land. These they quietly garrisoned. But they reckoned without another enemy worse than the foreign one. A number of active old ladies also occupied that zone at that particular period of history. If there was a war to be waged in their territory, they were well able to cope with their own end of it. Already they had, on many occasions and from time immemorial, triumphed over enemies, both foreign and domestic. They now appeared, in battle array, before Paddy Donncha Eoin and his half-company. Simultaneously with their ultimatum for the instant evacuation of all occupied buildings and terrain, they demonstrated the morale-shaking effect of vocal warfare. Paddy ordered an immediate retreat. Most of his men favoured that decision. Some few there were indeed who maintained that he should have stood his ground. But they were highbrows in the language movement. The old ladies' technique was, they declared, obsolete. Besides, they spoke only English and Irish. That limited their firepower. They, the highbrows, had studied American and other foreign languages, thus vastly increasing their effective volume. Nevertheless, they were prepared to admit that the Old Guard had done very well.

Now we appeared on the scene. I must say we got a very mixed reception. Excepting my soldier comrade, few of us had as yet much experience of war. I noticed that it was those with the least experience who were the most vociferous. They were also the most parochial-minded. They asserted that they were quite capable of dealing with any situation without any help foreign to the parish. We mildly replied that we were born three miles away on that hill to the south, which not so long ago was part of their parish. They gave us the assurance, many times reiterated, that no soldier was to be shot that day. They were to take the rifles from them without bloodshed. Now my comrade was, alas, a hard man, and I cannot therefore record his comments on this pronouncement. They further intimated that no fire-arms were to be used in the action. Making no reply we leaned our rifles against a convenient rock and, unbuckling our revolvers and ammunition slings, laid them down near them. We picked up two cudgels instead and, making ourselves comfortable on improvised seats inside the fence of the road, we waited. Presently their officer arrived and asked us to recover our revolvers and go to the extreme end of the position, to halt and disarm the officer leading the patrol. We took up these positions.

A scout on a bicycle arrived with the news that the patrol was on its way. He rode back towards the village and again returned with the news that they had left the main road and were now travelling on the road to Clondrohid, roughly parallel to ours and behind our backs. He remarked that we must wait for another day. We did not think so at all, as we knew that a mile or less across country would bring us to the Clondrohid road, where we could intercept them on their way back to Ballyvourney. The patrons of the cudgel claimed that the proposed ground was unsuitable for the use of their weapon, due to open spaces along the road. Here, some wag remarked that the day was not suitable either, that they should wait until next Fair Day. Eventually it was decided to send for seven or eight shotguns, and to man the nearest suitable stretch of road.

On our way over the hill we passed through Paddy Beag's

meadow; Paddy and another old man were at the hay. We must have numbered about twenty, between armed and unarmed men. It was a strange sight, in the middle of a fine harvest day, to see this body of young men pass through the field where two old men worked hard. Paddy thought so too, and told us so emphatically in Irish and English. His son Jer was with us. Under the lee of a group of us, Jer passed by his father unseen, while we replied cheerfully to Paddy's commentary. The fine day and the waste of labour seemed to be his principal trouble. We told him that it was a shame to be working on that fine day. Were it not that we had so much to do we would now make up the hay for him. Did he not know that we were all coming back in the near future, perhaps that very evening, to give him a hand? It would be advisable for him, therefore, to sit down and take things easy until we returned. This provoked his ironic laughter, and the last I heard of his satire as we streamed over the hill was something about 'idle cadays'.

From the northern slope of Cnoc an Iúir we looked down on the Clondrohid road. The vice-commandant of our battalion, Paddy O'Sullivan (Paddy Donncha Eoin), was with us, and the company area captain, Patsy Lynch. They held a council of war to which we were all admitted. No Volunteer was debarred from making a suggestion. That was one of the ways in which we differed from a regular army. We all looked down on the positions we were to occupy.

Each man, or group, was directed where to go. In the mean-time we would have to wait until two military lorries which had gone on to Ballyvourney returned. While we would be hidden from the patrol coming from the east, we could not remain unseen by anyone coming from the west.

We had to wait a long time for the return of the lorries. Waiting was always a strain. The thought inevitably recurred to the mind of the normal man of the tragedy of lying across the path of his fellow man, to cut short his life, or more or less maim him and cause him suffering. It did not require much intelligence to visualise that. The mind then asked why such a savage procedure was necessary. Well, in our case it was an effort to counter a long-established terror. Every other means had been tried. But still the tragedy persisted. The ordinary soldier, whom we would meet that day, was but the unwilling tool of the warmonger. There was nothing left for us to do but fight the tools, since we could not meet the masters. We would fight them as fairly as possible, but they would not have the advantage of the morning, their firearms versus our sticks.

The lorries passed by at 2 p.m. on their return journey to Macroom. With regret we let them go. With the garrison only a mile and a half away to the west and the patrol the same distance east of us, and with our poor armament, we could not do otherwise. We descended to the road and each group took the place allotted to them. The road from

Clondrohid, hardly the width of two cars, bent sharply around the Slippery Rock, which sloped upwards from its southern side. It was called the Slippery Rock by children coming home from school, who, seating themselves on flat stones, used to slide down its sloping face. It was now occupied by Paddy Donncha Eoin and three men with shotguns. Paddy had often slid down the Slippery Rock on his way home from school.

The road straightened out again for one hundred yards. Along its southern side there was no fence at that time. Along the northern side was a low fence and a few low little rocks. Behind these were disposed the remainder of the shotgun men and two with revolvers. At the extreme western end, and on the southern side, was a little hillock facing the approach road. Behind this hillock were stationed Mick the Soldier and I, with our two rifles. We had plenty of men besides, but had no guns for them. Free Kelleher put his eye on my Smith and Wesson revolver. I gave it to him. Then we settled down to another period of waiting. Some time, about 4 p.m., the scout on the hill above us signalled the approach of the patrol. We watched the bend at the Slippery Rock.

Riding at a steady pace they came, one by one, their officer leading them. They were like beads on a string set apart at the same intervals. They fitted exactly into the trap laid for them. The last man had rounded the bend. The officer was within thirty yards of us. Then we saw Paddy stand upright, his revolver in his hand, and loudly call on them to surrender. The officer looked back over his left shoulder. He said nothing but threw his weight on the pedals, put down his head and rode forward. All his men did likewise. There was no doubt about their intention. It was to break through. A revolver barked and a volley rang out. The officer fell but others came on. I jumped to my feet. We had been lying against the sloping face of the hillock. As I rose, a rifle exploded close to my left ear almost knocking me down again. It was Mick, who had risen before me and had fired across my back at some who were almost abreast of us. They were all down to cover or otherwise now. We stepped out on the road. There was another burst of rifle fire. We saw a soldier lying in the dust halfway down the road. He lay quite flat, his heels turned inwards, and was engaged in releasing rapid fire upwards at the top of the Slippery Rock. We fired simultaneously at him. Both bullets struck a foot apart under his body and raised a column of dust, which gave me the impression that we had cut his body in two. He let his rifle drop. Then there came silence.

The lads were coming out on the road. I walked past Jamie, Con Seán Jer and Ned Micky Sweeney as they disarmed a group of soldiers. One tall soldier struggled with Ned to retain his rifle. Ned wrenched it from him. I came to the man whom we had last fired at. He lay in exactly the same position, his left hand stretched in the firing posture and his right down on the road near the small of the butt. The rifle lay with a cartridge half thrust forward into the breech. His face was to the ground. I caught him by the shoulder and called, 'Hallo.' No reply. I thought him dead. My left hand grasping his right shoulder, I rolled him back. A fresh smiling face looked up at me out of humorous eyes.

'You are not dead,' I said.

'No,' he replied lazily.

'You are wounded or you ought to be.'

'I don't think so,' was the reply.

I opened his tunic, button by button. Not a scratch.

'I am very glad indeed,' I said.

'Thanks,' was his smiling reply.

The two bullets had torn deeply into the road under him as he lay. He had been lucky to escape the worst kind of wound.

I caught another by the shoulder as he lay face down on the grass of the northern dyke. He rolled over and put up his hands saying, 'Paddy, don't shoot!'

'We won't harm you,' I replied.

He unbuckled his equipment and handed it to me. I picked up his rifle and replaced it on his bicycle, with his steel cap and trench equipment. I saw Mick do the same. We had already settled on cycling home. A wounded soldier asked me for a cigarette. I had not a single one. I assured him I would get one for him. I tried all the lads. Not one.

Neither had any soldier one, I could do nothing but tell him how sorry I was.

The officer, Lieutenant Sharman, had been killed outright. Four soldiers had been wounded, not badly. All the arms, equipment and bicycles were collected. We were about to cycle home along the road to Clondrohid, as far as Drohidín Clia, then turn south for Kilnamartyra, when the scouts reported lorries from that direction. We had to take the bicycles on our shoulders up the steep side of Cnoc an Iúir.

John Harrington of Coolavokig now invited us to tea. We gladly accepted his invitation, since we had eaten nothing since 7.30 a.m. We left John's house soon after tea, for it was a likely place for an early raid. We descended the sloping fields of Coolavokig, to cross the main Macroom–Ballyvourney road at Yankee Lyons' gate. As we neared our crossing point we were in a slight hollow and for a minute or two lost sight of the road. In that short time two lorries from Macroom had turned the corner at Geata Bán unknown to us. Now they were quite near us and if we turned back we would be quite exposed to them. We ran towards the only cover, the two pillars of the gate of the field which we were in, and which opened onto the road almost opposite Yankee Lyons' gate. Yankee Lyons' wife stood in her own gateway and watched us make ourselves as small as possible behind the pillars across the road, while the lorries tore past to Ballyvourney with troops to search for the perpetrators of the Slippery Rock 'outrage'.

As we passed by Mrs Lyons, through the gateway she murmured fervently, 'The Lord save us, lads, the Lord save us!'

12

A HARVEST DAY IN 1920

A splendid morning about nine o'clock. I was alone at home in the village of Kilnamartyra (the Cross). My father came in.

'This is a very fine day, Micheál, and a likely one for a visit from those fellows.'

By 'those fellows' he meant two lorries of Auxiliaries who often paid us an unexpected visit. They had given us two close runs during the previous week. He added, 'You are all alone and my brother Patsy is threshing in Ballyvoig today. The devil a fear will they call there today or maybe ever call to the same place. You will have a fine peaceful day there.'

I took him at his word and went off to the threshing. Now, Ballyvoig, although but a mile due south of the Cross, was a 'lost valley'. It was near enough to everywhere and as near to Macroom as my own village, and yet no enemy of any description had set foot on it. All the inhabitants, including my Uncle Patsy, were honest, peaceful and law-abiding. By this it must not be inferred that a gangster was descending on them this peaceful morning. Not so, but that none of the young men of the valley was even a nominal Volunteer. One old man in the valley was enthusiastic about Ireland and helped every movement, military and otherwise, to set her free. His name was Jack Lehane. May he rest in peace, and all the others for that matter, for they ever hated to be disturbed.

Now as I descended the 'glittering hill' I could see in my uncle's haggard that all was ready to start. I turned in the gateway from the public road as if I came full of anxiety for work. Nor was I disappointed. My Uncle Patsy approached and, full of a genuine anxiety to get me working immediately, handed me a pike, saying, 'Go up on that stack there'.

'Very well,' I answered, and, taking the pike from him, stuck it in the ground. Quickly I removed my coat and, turning, walked back to where a horse side-car rested on its heels on the field just inside the gate.

As I turned I saw, and as I walked I felt, the impact of a score of eyes on my back. I knew the reason. As I entered the gateway I had looked fairly harmless. True, I wore the riding breeches and gaiters of the IRA, but that was not alarming. What was very alarming was the military equipment which the removal of my coat disclosed. A Sam Browne belt with two crossbelts and holsters which showed the butts of two

.45 Smith and Wesson service revolvers. Quickly I opened the waist belt and, removing the middle or top cushion of the side-car, I opened the 'well'. Into the 'well' went my guns and ammunition. Back went the cover and cushion, and, throwing my coat carelessly on top, I walked back to my pike. I plucked it up and started towards the stack indicated by my uncle. He lifted a warning hand. I stopped.

'Does your father know you are here today?'

'He sent me here.'

'My Gor.'

'What's wrong, Patsy?'

'Those things you brought, does he know you have them?'

'He does well.'

'Oh my!'

Raising my pike, I made a run to the stack and quickly reached the top.

From my point of vantage I had a full view of everything. It was a pleasant sight. The well-made stacks as yet untouched, but with a man on each poised for work. Around and on the thresher others stood ready. All watched the long belt between the steam engine and mill as it gathered speed. Soon the whine of the drum reached its peak and its music changed abruptly as the first sheaf went down. Then the steady tune again as the even feed was maintained. The work had started.

I waited for the man on the next stack to me and nearer

the thresher to remove the top. When he had made a level platform I started to throw the sheaves from my stack to his. He caught them and threw them onto the thresher platform. The work was easy. I enjoyed the exercise, the brilliant day, the general activity. I forgot Black and Tans, Auxiliaries and all disturbing things. I could see and sense that my neighbours working around me had forgotten me and that all were enjoying themselves. I was glad. I even regretted a little that I had come down into their happy valley and caused them perhaps not a little uneasiness. However, that, I reflected, was now forgotten and the chances of any enemy coming this way were very small.

Half an hour passed. I was now wholly engrossed in the work. It was very easy and pleasant. I passed the sheaves to my neighbour and he removed them at the same speed. Suddenly I became aware that I was gaining on him. He was not removing the sheaves. I glanced upwards. He had stopped. He had turned through a right angle and was gazing earnestly to the south and in a downward direction. I looked at the others. All in the high positions were in just the same posture. Soon all work ceased. I listened. I heard nothing but the even whine of the now idle drum. Then I heard from several, 'the Black and Tans' and 'Up the road' and again 'Two lorries!' Then I heard that then dreaded sound made by the engines and gears of the Crossley tenders. I knew where to look for them and where they were heading for.

There was only one road from the south and that was past the haggard gate.

The haggard was on a plateau overlooking the road along which they were coming. They would have to move along in front of us and beneath us for four hundred yards and distant three hundred yards from us. Then they would turn through a right angle and come sharply uphill to the haggard gate. There they would be higher than we and from the added height of the lorries would be looking down on us.

I saw them, first one, then the other fifty yards behind. They were coming fast on the level and were less than three hundred yards from the corner. The time was short. I had to make a quick decision.

In any other place there would have been only one course for me. I would have slipped off the stack, run to the sidecar, torn off the cushion and the cover of the well, taken the guns and perhaps leaving the coat which had nothing in its pockets, run back through the stacks to the cover of a fence with a hedge on top. This would safely lead me to rough ground where I would quickly be lost to them.

I took my eyes off the lorries. I had identified them. They were the Auxiliaries from Macroom Castle. A tough crowd. I knew them well. I had seen them jump walls with their rifles in their hands, hampered by their revolvers and other equipment. They travelled by night and day on byroads and came from totally unexpected directions. I had plenty of experience of their physical fitness, when I had to run from them on several occasions and when, were it not for darkness, they would have had me.

But here things were different. I looked from the lorries to the men who had been working with me. Now that they were sure, like myself, of the coming of hostile forces, they turned their eyes on me. One thing was certain, and that was that the haggard and every man in it would be searched. That would be the least misfortune. Worse might happen. If a man ran and was seen running, he was shot down. He could possibly be shot, too, for standing still. That was the order of the day. Nobody doubted it, not even the inhabitants of the 'lost valley'.

I looked at them. I knew them all. Most of them had gone to school with me. Not a Volunteer among them. All physically fit. A good few athletes among them. No good or harm in them, excepting some who covertly sneered at us. I thought of my comrades who had suffered and died and who were still doing so daily, and made a quick comparison. There was a great difference.

Suddenly I made up my mind. What were they watching me for? The time was getting very short. Ah, I knew. They were waiting for me to run. Of course. Now they would see this IRA man running out of sight before the lorries reached the gate. Then they would be model industrious citizens in the eyes of John Bull's terrorists and, of course, after being searched and interrogated, all would be well again. Very clearly in their eyes it was my duty to do the running.

I pushed my pike slowly down through the stack. I sat down carefully and slipped gracefully down. I walked at a dignified pace to the side-car, removed the cushion, the well cover, and took out my guns. I put them on like a coat and carefully closed the waist belt. All this I did in an unhurried manner and even delayed with the final adjustment of my coat. I was ready. I put back the well cover and cushion carefully, while my ears kept telling me how near was the enemy. I walked to the gateway and leaned my left shoulder against the pillar. Then I looked around at my fellow workers. It took them an appreciable time to realise that it was time for them to get busy again – that the time had come for *them* to run.

I heard the first change of gears and the increased whine of the leading lorry, then the snarl of the second change. I looked back to see how fared my fellow workers. I failed to see them. The bonnet of the leading lorry appeared. I noticed the engine failing. Then I saw the whole lorry and became aware of the battery of eyes on me. They drew abreast, and, just almost opposite me, the driver made the third change and stopped the car exactly opposite the gate. The road was narrow. The men and rifles towered and branched out over my head. Very carefully each man caught and held my eyes in turn. The first man nearest the driver raised his hand in salute, while still watching me intently. I returned the salute. He smiled. Then all the line saluted me. The driver raced his engine and they moved off again. My attention was now drawn from them to the second lorry. Exactly the same thing happened. The change of gears, the stop, the scrutiny, the salute, the smile at my salute and the general salute from all the men facing me. Then finally the tail of the second lorry disappearing around the corner.

I remained in the gateway, listening. I could tell by their gear changes all the steps and levels of the stair-like road to the top of Árd a' Bhóna. Then I turned about to meet the onset of my Uncle Patsy who, white-faced, again appeared on the stage. I veered towards the side-car while I removed my coat. The sight of the guns again restored his speech.

'Mighty save us above,' he gasped, 'things were not bad enough without going to the gate. What were you going to do if they came in, and what were we all going to do?'

'Ah, Patsy,' I said, 'they would not come in at all.'

'And what was to stop them?'

That finished my diplomacy. 'I was to stop them,' I replied sharply. 'Did you think or do you think now that I was going to run from that riff-raff? By the way, where are your own auxiliaries? Are you going to thresh your corn today?' I again put my guns in the 'well' with my coat on top and, running past him, climbed victoriously to the top of the stack. Seizing a pike again, I used it vigorously to add to the heap on my neighbour's stack. Then leaning on it, I watched with interest the gradual return of those who had 'studied their safety in flight'.

The work was resumed, the day passed, the corn was threshed. At teatime I heard, or rather overhead, about the dance. It was discussed in whispers, with furtive glances in my direction. I thoroughly understood. I had fitted badly into the scheme of things in Happy Valley. It was reasonable to assume that distance would considerably improve my relations with its inhabitants. Accordingly, when I announced that I was about to look for my cap to go home, I was forestalled by numerous volunteers who not only found my own cap for me, but several other caps as well. Relations had already shown a considerable improvement.

I walked uphill again on the road home. Reaching the first level, I stopped and looked back. It was dark and I could see nothing. I sat down on a mossy stone and lit a cigarette. I thought on the events of the day and especially on the recent anxiety to get rid of me. Resentment stirred in me. I got up to face homewards. The strains of music came to my ears. I turned downhill again.

The dance was being held at Jack Lehane's. There were three houses in the yard and it was his turn for that year.

I reached the door unnoticed. The kitchen was packed with dancers and men were standing close together just inside the doorway. The door was open. I stood looking in from the doorstep. After a while the set was finished. A pause. Then, I heard: 'We'll have a song from …'

Someone with perhaps some latent bit of patriotism started.

'Come tell me, Peter Crowley.'

I moved in, the better to hear that fine old ballad which I liked. *Aililiu,* as my grandmother used to say, I was seen! Soon I had plenty of room. They passed out in ones and twos beyond me. I was indeed the spectre at the feast.

In a short time I was seated beside Jack at the fire, discussing Ireland's wrongs and rights, with nothing to interrupt us save the crickets. At half-past ten I left him and started uphill again for the Cross.

13

THE FLYING COLUMN

The flying column in war is as old as war itself. It was used by armies, large and small, all over the earth, from the earliest times to the present day. It travelled on foot, horse or camel in the old days. In modern times it is mechanised and when airborne attains its true literal meaning. Its function remains always the same.

In guerrilla warfare, the flying column is the army. The more columns there are, and the more widely scattered they are, the longer will they last. I am, of course, assuming that the guerrilla forces are small and weak compared with those of their enemies. With such a discrepancy, it would be madness to gather together the forces of the weak and to pit them against those of the strong in one pitched battle. Common sense would indicate the wisdom of breaking up into small groups, each in its own native area and, by the judicious use of time and place, wage on the enemy a prolonged and harassing war. Such wars have been successfully fought. On such a pattern was fought the guerrilla war in Ireland which brought about the Truce with Britain in July 1921.

The flying column was a natural development of the resistance movement. The resistance movement started fitfully and spontaneously, then, in certain areas, it spread rapidly. The few men who started it were declared outlaws. To protect themselves from aggression and to maintain the resistance, they formed groups here and there. These groups became the bases of the flying columns. This was the case in our district, the military designation of which was the 8th Battalion area. It was part of the Cork No. 1 Brigade area, which included Cork city and the middle of the county to the Kerry border. Early in the autumn of 1920 we had a battalion column of thirty men. All were well armed with rifles and revolvers, which had been taken from the enemy. All were first-class marksmen.

Early in January 1921 the brigade flying column was formed. It was achieved by adding fifteen men from Cork city to our battalion column. The brigade flying column was not a good idea, but it was a matter of expediency, since few areas could arm a battalion column. Had the supply of arms been adequate, men to use them would not have been lacking. Then the brigade would have had eight columns instead of one. Each would operate on its own ground and, knowing it thoroughly well, would make the best use of it. If one column got into difficulties, there would be a great possibility of its receiving timely assistance from one or more of its neighbours. The opportunities for attacking and harassing the enemy would have been increased a hundredfold.

The brigade column had little to recommend it. It had much too large an area to deal with successfully. Often it was found that, after a forced march of twenty miles or more, the journey had been made in vain. Such disappointments were, in fact, only too common. But the most serious disadvantage of all was the ever-present danger of encirclement by overwhelmingly powerful forces. The column was only a unit moving about alone over a wide area. Had a second or third unit also moved, at least some confusion and doubt would have been caused among the enemy's intelligence system. But it is comparatively easy to keep track of a single unit, when once sighted. Thus, it often happened that a column, alarmed at dawn, found itself in a circle of steel.

For instance, once our column had returned to one of its bases in western Ballyvourney. We had rested there for two days. The time was March 1921. Quite suddenly, just before nightfall, we got an order to move. It was merely a precautionary measure. Our officers considered that we had been long enough in that glen and, to nullify the efforts of enemy agents, we would now move to new ground. Despite the difficulties attached to their use, we always brought two powerful touring motor cars along with us. Into them we now stowed our impedimenta, blankets, light mattresses, grenades and other heavy gear. With the Lewis-gun section I travelled in one. The column moved off across the hills, while we, taking advantage of the twilight to drive without lights, went by quiet roads around the feet of the hills. Our destination was Carraig Bán, a deep secluded glen in Ballingeary.

As we threaded our way through the long, narrow and tortuous boreen leading to the farmhouse, our headquarters, we had to use our headlamps. Knowing the formation of the glen and its surrounding hills so well, the use of the lights gave us no cause for anxiety. We entered the farmyard and left the cars near two big heaps of *aiteann gaolach*, the light species of furze used as bedding or litter. Soon we were seated in front of a mighty fire in the big kitchen, while the two daughters of the house, splendid girls, made tea for us. Some of the more chivalrous of the young men of the column hastened to assist at the operation, while others advised the girls not to accept their services but to relegate them to some menial work like the bringing in of turf, the sweeping of the yard or the cleaning of the stalls. A most enjoyable crossfire of wit ensued and for a while the house shook with laughter.

The tea over, arrangements for sleeping accommodation, the guard for the night, sentries and communications were made. A large barn, its timber floor swept clean, was available. On the floor the column placed its portable mattresses. Sometimes, if it did not inconvenience the people and a spare room or two was available, a number of us stayed in the dwelling house. This was the case on this night, as the people of the house insisted on it. The arrangements completed, some of the column went off to nearby houses with local Volunteers for a few hours, while some returned to the fire in the kitchen. Here we passed the time pleasantly with song and story until nearly midnight. With the Lewis-gun section, a few of the column and a visiting brigade officer, I shared a room upstairs. Our quarters were most comfortable and soon we were fast asleep.

The sound of heavy rifle fire must have awakened us simultaneously, for we were all on our feet in one movement. It was morning and the sun shone brightly. Jim Grey was singing as he reached for his clothes.

Hurrah, boys, the morning of battle has come!
And the *générale* is beating on many a drum.
They rushed from their revels to join the parade,
For the van is the right of the Irish Brigade!

'Take off my gaiters again,' I ordered the quartermaster, who was stouter than I and who had nearly succeeded in fastening the last buckle of the pair. With a laugh he complied and I handed him his own pair. We dashed downstairs and out to the yard where our officers were marshalling the column. Already scouts had been sent uphill to the north to try and find a way out. The enemy had come into the glen from the east and south. Our sentries had retired before them. No column man had been hit.

We started to climb the steep hill to the north. We were aided by a *cumar* or bed of a stream which had worn deeply into the hillside. The enemy kept up an irregular fire but their shooting was bad. We did not reply to it. The enemy behind us was not worrying us. We were thinking of the enemy in front who might, at any moment, appear almost vertically over us on the brow of the hill. This, however, did not happen, and we reached the top without incident. We found ourselves on a bare moor, entirely devoid of cover, and which stretched for miles to the north and west. We also found that we were very far from being out of trouble. We watched enemy troops swarm behind us from the south and east. A scout now appeared from the north-east who reported that troops, including Auxiliaries, were due north of us and moving westwards along the ridge of Maoileann.

The open plain in front of us now was our greatest obstacle. We dared not move across it. Had it been broken ground of any kind, or with even heather on it, we could have kept moving on. Could we reach the fringe of the circle and good fighting ground we would have a fair chance of breaking through or of holding out until dark. A new enemy appeared, a low-flying plane. We could clearly see the pilot and observer as they swooped repeatedly down on us. Sometimes, when they circled they were actually under us as they swooped into the glen we had left. The column lay in a circle, quite flat and motionless on the short mountain grass. A little rock, heather covered, jutted out of the ground nearby. It had one straight face, about five feet high. I stood by that face, the Lewis gun mounted on top. I merged well into the landscape. Each time the plane passed I followed it with the gun sights. I knew the technique of firing at it. It was a cock-shot in any case. The plane came so often and travelled so accurately over us that I expected it would machine-gun us. I decided to anticipate it and glanced back at the column leader. He shook his head and spoke.

'We can't do it, Mick, that cursed place out there would ruin us.' He referred to the bare ground ahead of us. The plane came round again, nearer than ever. I again glanced backwards. The column leader came and stood beside me, his hand on my arm.

'The lives of all the lads would be in danger,' he said. Then turning to the other officers he asked each in turn if it were not better to keep quiet. All agreed that it would be the wiser course, excepting my brother Pat, who thought that the plane was preparing to open fire on us. The matter was settled by a sudden change in the weather. The sun which had shone brightly was darkened by a cloud, a blanket of fog came down on us and rain began to fall. We saw no more of the plane or of any other enemy. To make sure that he had gone we pushed westward across the open ground to a point where we could look down on the glen. The weather cleared, the sun shone again and we could see to great distances. There was no sign of an enemy and we descended to the house. As we drew near it we could see into the farmyard. Our two cars had disappeared.

When we were leaving the yard that morning we sadly realised that, whatever hope we had of extricating ourselves from the round-up, there was no possibility of taking the cars. The boreen ended where they had been left. At the door of the house we met the two girls. They were in high glee.

'They did not find the cars!' was their first greeting.

Our astonishment changed to delight and unbounded admiration as we heard the story those great girls told us.

After our hurried departure the girls had seized two forks and pulled down the heaps of furze on the cars. Working feverishly they had covered them completely and had done their heavy task so well that we who had already seen the rough heaps never suspected that they now enclosed our transport. Troops had swarmed into and around the house and out-offices. They entered the barn, but the column had long practice at leaving no trace of occupation, however hurried their departure. One mystery there was for which

Dan T. MacSweeney (Kilnamartyra Company) and his wife Mary, sister of the author and Captain/organiser of Kilnamartyra Cumann na mBan.

John Con Cronin, Captain of Ballingeary Company.

Donncadh MacNeilus (Dún na nGall), Division Vice-O/C Engineering.

Volunteer Christy Lucey (Cork city), shot dead by Auxiliaries at Túirín Dubh, aged 22.

Éamon Mac Suibhne, Captain of Coolea Company, after his release from prison in 1921. He was tortured on his capture and returned home sick and emaciated. He died aged 29.

Some members of Coolea Company.
Front row: Dan Sullivan, Jamie Moynihan. *Second row:* Éamon Mac Suibhne, Neilus Moynihan, Michael Sullivan. *Third row:* Micheál Mac Suibhne. *Back row:* Nonie Moynihan.

Some members of Ballyvourney Cumann na mBan with section leader Liam Hegarty. *Front row from left:* Minnie Twomey and Bridge Dineen, Ballymakeera; Ms MacSweeney, Gort na Scairte; Margaret Ní Shuibhne, Múirneach Beag. *Back row from left:* Maud Collins, Ballymakeera; Maria O'Riordan, Seana Chluain; Kathy Hegarty and Leena Lucey, Ballymakeera; Mae Lynch, Ullanes; Liam Hegarty, Ballymakeera.

Dónal Óg Ó Ceallacháin, Sinn Féin Lord Mayor of Cork from 1920–23. He was elected after the death, on hunger strike, of Terence MacSweeney on 25 October 1920.

John Patrick Cronin,
Ballingeary Company.

Volunteer Ian McKenzie Kennedy
(Scotland), killed in action in
Rochestown, Cork city, aged 23.

Paddy Donncha Eoin
O'Sullivan, Vice-O/C 8th
Battalion, 1st Cork Brigade.

Seánín Donncha Eoin O'Sullivan,
Ballyvourney Company, brother of
Paddy.

Left to right: Micheál Ó Súilleabháin (author), Dan 'Farmer' Harrington and Dónal Óg Ó Ceallacháin *c.* 1932.

RIC Auxiliaries using bloodhounds to track members of the IRA *c.* 1920–21. *Courtesy of Mercier Press.*

Micheál Ó Súilleabháin driving Éamon de Valera in Cork city, 1924.

The courthouse and barracks at the Mills, Ballyvourney.

The Glebe House, Inchigeela. Burned on 2 June 1920 due to impending occupation by British forces.

British troops on a Crossley tender in Inchigeela, County Cork. The Lake Hotel (*left*) and Corcoran's (now Creedon's) Hotel (*right*) were barricaded and occupied by enemy forces.

Micheál Ó Súilleabháin, Kilnamartyra Company.

Eugene (Hugie) O'Sullivan, Coolea Company.

Jim Grey (Cork city), O/C Brigade transport.

Macroom Castle, County Cork, which housed a company of RIC Auxiliaries during the War of Independence.

we could never offer an explanation. That was the matter of the tracks of our cars. That the tracks were there, plain to be seen, from the main road to the yard is beyond doubt. And what is equally certain is that no question was asked about the tracks.

There was no mystery about the enemy's early morning descent on Carraig Bán. Arrangements had long been made for a concentric and overwhelming attack on the column. It had already been tried at Coolnacahera with dire results for the Auxiliaries of Macroom: now every garrison had been waiting for the word which would give the exact position of its target. It came at last, Carraig Bán, Ballingeary. The enemy's machinery worked swiftly and smoothly. But our brigadier's foresight caused their well-laid scheme to go 'agley'. We had hardly reached Carraig Bán when he ordered off a group of local Volunteers to block the Pass of Céimaneigh. Early in the morning enemy forces from Bantry were still vainly trying to break through the Pass when they should have been in position above Carraig Bán to greet us as we toiled up the hill.

The Auxiliaries from Macroom passed through Rena- nirree and Béal a' Ghleanna early in the morning. Meeting with people on the way they inquired for the road to Carraig Bán. They got the reply that there was no such place. Nevertheless, they pushed on to the place indicated on the map. Johnny Lynch of Béal a' Ghleanna was in his kitchen talking to a neighbour, who had brought a horse and cart for some piece of machinery. Johnny had a huge dog, which started to bark furiously outside. Fearing that he would attack some visitor Johnny hastened out. A tall man armed with rifle and revolver and wearing a trench coat was coming downhill to the house. The dog was disputing the ground with him. Johnny called off the dog and waited, while he tried to assess the identity of the stranger. The man wore a Glengarry cap but that did not condemn him, as Johnny knew that the column possessed a few of them. He was smiling as the man drew near. The man spoke and Johnny knew he was an Auxiliary.

'Come along with me!' the Auxie said. 'Stop that dog! You come too!'

He addressed Johnny's neighbour who had come to the door. The three went down to the road where they met a group of Auxiliaries. Their officer questioned both Johnny and his neighbour. He told them he would take them both as hostages for the day. Johnny said he did not mind going with them if he got a little time to release the cows from their stalls, as there was no one at home to do so. The officer said he should ask the major and perhaps he would allow Johnny to remain at home, but the neighbour should go with the group. He took Johnny with him to find the major. As they went uphill away from the house it started to rain. Johnny had no coat and the officer fastened a ground sheet around his shoulders. It was a kindly act, which belied a gruff manner and rough exterior. Soon they met the major with another group. He spoke roughly to Johnny.

'Who are you, and where did you get that sheet?'

Johnny's companion answered for him and explained that there would be no one after him at home to feed cattle and do other necessary work. The major agreed to allow him to go home. The pair returned to the group on the road. As the group moved off Johnny's neighbour asked him to take his horse home when he got a chance of doing so. Johnny assured him that it would be done.

Returning home, Johnny drove the cows up the hill behind the house. On the way he passed a Lewis-gun section of the Auxies. They challenged him and asked him how he was allowed up there. He replied that he had got permission from the major. They motioned him on. On his way down, impelled by curiosity to get a closer view of the gun position, he passed nearer to the group. One of them spoke, a sinister ring in his voice.

'If I were you, I would keep away.'

Without comment, Johnny moved on past that treacherous crowd and soon reached the house. Untying the neighbour's horse he sat in the car and drove him home. The big dog followed him. His road was down the glen, which was dotted with groups of military and Auxiliaries. He was not molested until he had disposed of the horse and had started to walk home. Despite his best endeavours he could not avoid meeting a group. They immediately questioned him. He told them he had been released by the major, but they said that made no difference, that he should come with them. He went with them and after a time they released him. He again faced for home and was taken by a new group. This particular company did not display any interest in his movements, but were deeply concerned about the welfare of the big handsome dog. They said the poor 'blighter' was hungry and should be fed, and set about doing so with generous portions of their rations. Some said he was not fat enough and should be fattened up immediately, while others alleged that he was over fat. When the dog had eaten enough they released Johnny and, with great reluctance, the dog.

* * *

One's thoughts travel back along the roads and paths we used to know so well as we moved here and there among the people. In reality it meant only moving from one home to another. Very often the people we stayed with had sons in the column or Volunteers, or daughters in Cumann na mBan. But in any case we were always welcome and they gave us what they often denied themselves. If we happened to stay in a glen or valley for even three or four days, the young people, boys and girls, organised a dance or concert in our honour. If there was a wake or funeral we always attended if the opportunity was favourable. In short, we belonged to the people.

One night a group of us attended a wake in one of our favourite glens. Sentries had been posted for the night, and the danger of surprise was very little. We entered the house of mourning an hour before midnight, said our prayers and sympathised with the people of the house. The old man who had died had lived to a fine old age, so, while his people and the neighbours regretted his passing, there was none of the sorrow associated with the loss of youth. We sat down among the neighbours and in low voices we discussed the old man's struggle with life, his triumphs and his virtues. Soon the hour of midnight was upon us, the signal for the recitation of the Rosary. The head of the household came into the kitchen and, meeting a near neighbour, asked him to lead in the recital of the prayers. He at once agreed to do so and forthwith dropped on his knees. People gathered from all over the house to the kitchen or its immediate vicinity. They knelt on the floor, which was covered with immense flag-stones, hard and fairly uneven. Truly a floor from which one's knees could hope for little mercy. Chairs were given to the old upon which they could rest their forearms and thus afford themselves some relief.

I had noticed that, when the leader of the prayers had accepted that position, something like a sigh of resignation had arisen from the people. It had never occurred to me, at the time, that it could possibly have been a sign of disapproval or even of despair. For the individual selected was well known in the district as a hard taskmaster in the matter of public prayer. Moreover, some of the more outspoken alleged that he was a mere humbug, a petty dictator, a tyrant who, like Cromwell, used his long prayers as a medium of persecution. Hard words, no doubt. Others held that his was a mere human failing, that once set in motion, his own volition was insufficient to bring him to rest within a reasonable period of time. In any case, he had now started.

I noticed that he prayed in English, although such prayers were invariably said in Irish in that district. To my left and in front of me knelt my friend Old John. He gave the responses in Irish. Old John was nearly eighty years of age. Nobody would dream of calling him a humbug. He was well known and respected as an upright man, honest and outspoken. I was soon to see his patience tested.

Our leader started off with a prayer of his own which immediately awoke in me a sense of irritation. I suspected, perhaps wrongly, that he wished to impress us with his superior knowledge and greater rectitude. He then recited the Apostle's Creed, after which he proceeded with the regular Rosary, the Salve Regina and the Litany. These beautiful prayers were responded to with reverent attention, as was the long Prayer for the Dead. The usual number of prayers had by this time been exceeded, but as yet the people showed no signs of weariness. I pitied Old John who still knelt unmoved on the hard sandstone. Another litany started and was completed in due course, which to us appeared a long time. I noticed Old John showing signs of discomfort. He tried, by various movements of his limbs and body, to ease his cramped position. But he got no respite. Another prayer was said, and yet another. By then the youngest amongst us was feeling badly, and what must Old John have been suffering! At last the end came, and that violently. We had hoped that the finish of the last prayer would be the end of all, but alas!

'We will now say five Our Fathers and five Hail Marys for the suffering souls in Purgatory.'

But he never said them. There were other poor souls suffering on earth who thought that the people in Purgatory were relatively well off.

I heard the screech of the chair legs as Old John thrust it forward to make room for himself. Pressing downwards with both his hands on the seat he struggled to his feet. His eyes blazing with fury, he faced his persecutor.

'In the Name of God and stop,' he shouted. 'When they'll be tired of having them inside, they'll let them out!'

14

COOLNACAHERA
AND COOMNACLOHY

The column left the old house at Clountycarty at an early hour, sometime about 6 a.m. It was the morning of 25 February 1921. They had left about the same time every morning for the past fortnight, and returned at the same time when night fell. But the old house would be lonely again tonight without their songs and merry laughter, for they were destined not to return. Their route was the same as that of the previous mornings, north-east across country, first through the bogs of Gurtanedin, across the Renanirree road, upwards through Clohina of the stunted oak and holly groves, down Cappanahilla, along a boreen, past a disused farmhouse, along by hedges to cross the inches to the Sullane. Across the Sullane by Tom Murray's steps, and cautiously upwards and fanning outwards, to occupy a quarter-mile stretch of the Macroom–Ballyvourney road, at Coolnacahera.

The column crossed the road to the northern side and occupied the full length of the ambush position. A small column from the 7th or Macroom Battalion occupied the only suitable positions on the southern side. I was in charge of the Lewis gun for the time being, Hugie having gone home the night before. He was due back any minute. However, I laid the gun ready for action and then had a look about me. I was alone in a natural depression on top of a rock that commanded a wide field and a long stretch of road. On my left was John Patrick (Cronin), number three in our Lewis-gun section, next to him Pat Mary Walsh (Cronin), and next to Pat, John McCann MacSweeney, all sharp-shooting riflemen from Ballingeary. On my left front I could see Corney O'Sullivan, Jim Grey, Seán Murray, Patsy Lynch, my brother Pat, Sandow and Jack Culhane. I could see that the Macroom men were in their positions across the road.

It was a morning of bright sunshine and clear air with a little frost, and a stillness which made sound audible at a great distance. Suddenly I became aware of a complete silence. Everyone I could see appeared to be listening intently. At first I could hear nothing. Then I thought I heard a very faint singing noise. Soon I heard it distinctly but thought it came from a great distance. I wondered whether our signaller was yet at his post. We were hardly ten minutes in position. Then I heard, 'Mick, Mick!', from my brother Pat's group. They also motioned me to cover and a low voice added: 'They are coming!'

I relayed the message across the road to Dan Corkery and his men, and also to number four section behind my back.

My eyes ran along the straight to where the surface of the road disappeared at the bend, then across a loop to where it appeared again, and there they were. I counted as they passed. A touring car with seven lorries behind it, close together. But they were coming very, very slowly. There was something wrong. I lay down behind the gun. Would they ever reappear? I brought the butt to my shoulder and glanced along the sights to the corner. I took off the safety-catch. The touring car appeared. At little more than a snail's pace it came until it was clear of the corner. Then the leading lorry hove in sight. They must be very suspicious, nevertheless they edged forward. The second was in sight. The occupants, Auxiliaries, were standing as if ready to jump off the while they scrutinised the ground ahead of them. The third lorry appeared. I heard a noise behind me. Hugie lay down beside me. I slipped sideways from him saying: 'Take that.'

'Weren't you doing all right,' he said.

He put the butt to his shoulder and sighted. Two shots rang out at the eastern end of our positions. Hugie pressed the trigger.

The 'glen serene' was now awake with a vengeance. The

guns were pealing with a joyous abandon. It was a place of echoes, and one got the impression that other battles raged in the distance at every point of the compass. The sound struck the rocky face of Rahoona a mile away to the south-west and returned undiminished. An old man travelling a path along its side stooped in terror at the mouth of a *béilic* to get cover. A fox jumped from a rock onto his back and vanished into the cave. On Rahoona and away to the south on the hills of Kilnamartyra, people congregated to hear if not to see the battle. An athletic and somewhat poetic young man of military age remarked to my mother, 'Is there not something inspiring in the crack of the rifle?'

'There is indeed,' she replied, 'when one is a good distance away from it.'

But I must return to the fight. The Auxiliaries had heard of our trap for them. There was plenty of evidence of this. As the lorries approached our position, four hostages were ordered out to walk ahead of them. We saw them and realised what they were. Bullets passed them by to strike down Auxiliaries near them, but the hostages remained unhurt. When the first burst of fire struck the car and lorries, both Auxiliaries and hostages dived for shelter. One of the prisoners got in over a low fence south of the road.

'Get out again,' said an Auxie, presenting a revolver. The Auxie fell dead.

'Come over here,' said another Auxie. 'Lie down there,'

he said, 'don't go out. We'll get those fellows after a while. They have got only revolvers.'

The Lewis gun spoke again.

'By G–,' said the Auxie 'the b—s have got the quick-firing so-and-so's.'

Everyone who saw the enemy coming could see that they knew they were nearing the spot where we were. Whether they actually saw something or someone near the extreme eastern or Macroom end of our position is a matter of doubt. At any rate two of them jumped off one of the slow-moving lorries and rushed up a heather-covered rock on the northern side. They were shot down. Those two shots, of course, set the ball rolling. Had they crept forward another two hundred yards, they would have been under fire from the whole column. As it happened, less than twenty men were engaged with them north of the road, while south of the road the Macroom men were fewer.

The halting of the enemy did much, of course, to rob us of a speedy and complete victory. That was but the fortune of war and we cannot blame the Auxiliaries for acting on the information they had got that we were waiting for them. But the frailty of a member of the column did far more that day to weaken our blows and at the same time strengthen the enemy. I am now referring to the unspeakable 'X'. He was responsible, a few weeks later, for the horrible murder of six of his comrades at Clogheen. That the creature who brought the murder and torture gang to fall on his sleeping comrades did so to save himself is the most just and charitable thing I can say about him. For some argue that he had already started on his fiendish work as an informer. Certainly he had been over-inquisitive about the names of people and places while with the column, but that proves nothing. The poor wretch has enough to his account anyway, without adding to it, and I pray God that his like may not be there again.

A few weeks before this day, Jim Grey and I, after considerable labour with indifferent tools, had fitted out and tested another Lewis gun. We had hoped to be allowed to use it in action against the enemy. We were astonished when 'X' got charge of it, for nearly all of us doubted his integrity. So it was that, when the first shots were fired, 'X', stationed near the extreme end, was in a position to wreak the utmost destruction on the enemy massed under him.

But, leaving the gun, he ran, and demoralised others around him. A young lad, Dick Kingston from Ballyvourney, picked it up and brought it away. I used it afterwards and found it excellent. 'X' alleged that it failed to work for him in the morning.

Across the road from the 'X' position were two labourers' cottages. They stood about forty yards apart and were screened from the road by a stone fence. Their acre plots were also enclosed by a similar fence. The cottages and plots were on a hillock which sloped to the south and west. The Auxiliaries had no option but to retire into and defend this ground when they were driven off the road. The Macroom men were admirably posted to prevent them escaping or fighting their way to the south or west, and admirably well they did their task. Not alone did they hold them in the plots, but finally their steady and accurate fire drove them uphill to the immediate environs of the cottages. A few men with Neddy Neville of Rusheen occupied a hillock, the most easterly point of the Macroom men's positions. Once the Auxiliaries contemplated taking them in the rear. Keeping away to the east, they started to creep south. Neddy shot down the leader and that finished the project.

I believe the first two shots were fired by John Riordan (Jack the Rookery) and Jer Casey (Strac). They had no other option since the two Auxiliaries rushed up to their positions. The Lewis gun and about twenty rifles opened fire on the Auxies while most of them were still on the lorries, and though they quickly sought cover many fell on the road and along the dykes. Seafield Grant, the officer commanding the Macroom Auxiliaries, escaped the first fire. Standing on a patch of green south of the road, he gazed north-west towards the rocks. Two bullets scored tracks in the sod in front of him. Stooping, he examined the scars. Straightening up, he looked back along the direction indicated by them. A third bullet came which killed him. His fall must have disheartened the enemy very much. At first their fire was vigorous. Bullets struck the flat surface of vertical rocks with a loud thud, or curved high into the air with a wailing note when a sloping rock-face was hit. A Hotchkiss gunner appeared to have an idea of the location of our Lewis. His shooting was getting better, and when it cracked over our heads for a while Hugie said to me, 'Keep a look out for that fellow.'

At length we located him, as Hugie said, 'just below Diarmaid na gComharsan's cottage'. One sharp burst from the Lewis and the gunner, frightened or hit, dragged the gun backwards. We did not hear any more from him. The Auxiliaries' fire weakened and now and then a man or two made a dash for the cottages. We also saw other indications that they were hard pressed. One of the lorries was being turned about on the road by the driver. A fierce fire was opened on it. It got away, however, and went off at a high speed towards Macroom. The driver was a stout fellow and made skilful use of available cover while he quickly completed the manoeuvre.

We could now expect their reinforcements. It transpired that they were on the way in any case. Meanwhile, the Auxies were crowding into the cottages. To make more fire positions, they started to break loopholes in the cottage walls. For this they used every kind of tool available, including their bayonets. The loopholes were to prove, for them, very unprofitable. For, immediately the outer plaster was broken, the hole in the wall became the target for every marksman who fancied himself. Several Auxies were mortally wounded inside these breaches.

We were now called on to follow up the enemy and move with the Lewis gun to a point due north of the cottages. This we did easily. The windows and doors were now under our fire and that of about fifteen riflemen. The Auxiliaries were in a bad way. Their total strength of the morning must have been nearly ninety men. Apart from those strewn around the road and further afield as casualties, the remainder were packed into the two cottages and lying close to cover around outside them. Now and again a man would rise and dash for the door. But no man succeeded in getting in. We saw an Auxie fall on the doorstep wounded. Yet no one attempted to drag him in. To do so would have entailed no risk for those inside since our fire was parallel to that particular doorway, yet there he was allowed to remain.

We stood in a line along a fence. Every grenade we had was in a man's hand. We were ready for the final dash at them. Then suddenly we heard an exclamation from Seán O'Hegarty.

'Look lads, look!'

He raised his Parabellum pistol and fired. An unbroken line of lorries extended far away to the east. The new enemy, thirty-six lorries strong, had come in time to save the Auxiliaries. For a little time while they were massed together, we fired at them. Then slowly we drew away to the high ground north of us. It was midday when we left them. The action had started at 7.45 a.m. As we moved uphill we felt very disappointed. We had been very near victory despite many agencies working against us. First, the enemy had been forewarned and arrangements had been made to send reinforcements from all quarters. Then someone had blundered in the handing over of a vital position and a powerful weapon, to the incompetent and wretched 'X'. Again there was the case of a section leader who, though highly efficient in a town, could not understand the prolonged action and, thinking they were being encircled, withdrew a large number of the best men of the column. Thus was our striking force much weakened and valuable time lost.

Looking at the bright side of the picture, the small number engaging the Auxiliaries had proved more than a match for these warriors. Only six miles from their base, the strong castle of Macroom, they had that day the heartening assurance of reinforcements converging on us from Cork and Ballincollig, Bandon, Dunmanway, Bantry, Killarney, Millstreet and Macroom. We had fired on these reinforcements before we broke off the fight and were destined to clash with more within two hours. We had no reserve forces to come to our relief. Our only hope lay in a speedy action and a retreat in the right direction, before the net could be closed. Nevertheless, before we left, the Auxies were quiet boys. Fourteen had been killed and twenty-six wounded. Half of them, roughly, were out of action, and it was only the certainty of relief that caused the remainder to hang on. We had no casualties. We had, therefore, much to be thankful for.

We crossed over Cnoc an Iúir and descended to Ullanes valley. Turning west, we ascended Ullanes hill and kept along its ridge until we came down to cross the mountain road from Ballyvourney to Millstreet. A branch of this road runs into the glen of Coomnaclohy. Here, in this cul-de-sac from a military point of view, the city men of the column insisted on stopping for a cup of tea at Dinneens' farmhouse. My brother Pat strongly opposed this proposal. He pointed out to their leader that, while his men could hardly be taken from the rear, a sudden invasion by lorry-borne troops would compel them to ascend the steep sides of the glen where there was difficult footing and little cover. Taking the Lewis-gun section with him, he went up to Muing Lia where from a height we could look down from the west on the valley we had just crossed.

We went into the farmhouse and soon we were seated at a table, very much at our ease and about to enjoy a cup of tea, which a young girl had just poured for each of us. Nine hours had passed since we had had our breakfast. Over forty years have passed since I saw that cup of tea poured out and I have forgotten many things, but I can still see that. I put sugar in it and I had the jug in my hand to put milk in it. But that was as far as I got. I had been looking through the window, which was straight in front of me. Away to the south-east I could see a white ribbon of road. I saw a speck appear on it, then another and another. They were coming, one behind the other.

'What do you think those are?' I asked the girl, indicating to her the road.

With the teapot clasped between her hands, she regarded them.

'I think they are bicycles,' she replied. Still watching them, she said again, 'No, they are lorries.'

They were lorries, sure enough. We went outside, the better to investigate.

The lorries were on the Top Road, which runs on high ground to the north of Ballyvourney village and parallel to the main road to Killarney. They were coming down to the junction with the mountain road to Millstreet. Would they turn down to the Mills, Ballyvourney? If they did we could return to our tea. But they did not turn left for Ballyvourney. They turned right and came up the Millstreet road. There was still a chance. Would they turn right below Seán Hyde's and go on to Millstreet? They did not. They kept left and came on into Coomnaclohy.

We ran forward to a high meadow where we could be seen from the farmhouse below. I whistled with my fingers.

Someone came out. We pointed down to the road. They all came out of the house and we signalled them forward and then to cover behind a fence. They lined the fence, but my brother said he would go down to them.

'If anything goes wrong,' he said, 'the city lads may go the wrong way out of that hole.'

Instructing us to keep an eye on the Killarney road behind us, he ran downhill from us. Meanwhile, the lorries came on. They carried soldiers of the regular army. Our men had lined a fence parallel to the road and back a few hundred yards. The lorries stopped on the road opposite them. They must have seen someone. I saw one of our men stand up just before they stopped. At any rate, they dismounted and deployed as if on field exercise. Rapidly advancing, they reached the middle of the field. Our men opened fire. The enemy fell flat and returned a volley. Then rising, they again rushed forward. I noticed that they had yet no casualty. Their flanks were extended beyond our line and they greatly outnumbered our men, who began to withdraw and shoot in like manner. The shooting on both sides was equally bad. Now our men had to face the hill and were doing so in the worst possible way. Here my brother intervened and directed them into a *cumar*, or bed of a stream, which ran slantwise to the enemy and so gave shelter. With a few men he held back the enemy while the others mounted. The enemy continued to fire but did not attempt to follow up. When they reached us Corney asked why we had not fired over their heads with the Lewis. We replied that we could have done little or no damage at that range to the extended enemy, and might have caused confusion among some of our own men coming uphill. Three soldiers were wounded in this skirmish and one of our men got a very slight wound in the hand. While the shooting lasted and for some time afterwards, enemy lorries stood a few miles south of us on the Killarney road. Had they had the will to do so, they could actually have driven up behind us.

The Dunmanway Auxiliaries arrived at Kilnamartyra, a few miles south of Coolnacahera, early in the forenoon, while fighting was in progress. From several hilltops they viewed the scene and listened to the firing. Instead of going straight towards it by a very direct road which would have brought them out at Poul na Bró, just where they were wanted on the western flank of the column, they continued westward to Renanirree, four miles away. Turning north, they went in the general direction of Ballyvourney, but by the most intricate network of byroads. They arrived there, of course, in time to be late, but that does not appear to have depressed them unduly. Indeed, at one of their stops in Kilnamartyra, one of them was heard to remark that they would be there quite soon enough. An unarmed man running away from them would perhaps have roused their enthusiasm. Like their comrades who waited on the Killarney road, the noise of battle did not appeal to them. Fifty-two lorries of regulars and Auxiliaries were present at or near the scene of battle at noon. Excepting the troops that entered Coomnaclohy, the others did not show any great desire to follow up the column. Instead they chose a more congenial occupation. They burned the two cottages that had sheltered the Auxiliaries, a neighbouring hayshed and two farmhouses. North of Ballyvourney village they shot down an unarmed Volunteer, severely wounding him.

The day was not without its humour. Paddy Beag and another old man were behind the rocks at Coolnacahera, unconscious of any impending disturbance. Suddenly the firing started and deflected bullets whined high over them. At their highest speed they started towards home. Presently, in comparative safety, they stopped to draw their breath.

'Isn't it an awful thing, Paddy, to see two oul' lads like us having to run like this. Or what is the country coming to?'

'It is then,' said Paddy, 'but these times won't last always. God is good.'

'Ah,' said the other old man, 'sure I know He's good, *but what can He do?*'

Liam Jer was an old man whose legs were somewhat reduced in efficiency by the march of time, but whose peculiar wit and tongue flourished unimpaired. He lived in a small farmhouse on the side of the narrow road from Poul na Bró to Kilnamartyra. The rocky and steep Rahoona hill cast its shadow, in the evening, on Liam's hacienda. We scarcely ever passed by without meeting Liam.

'*Conus tá'n sibh. Bhfuil aon oul' news agaibh?*' was always his greeting.

He took the greatest pleasure in answering questions put to him by enemy forces. This evening Liam met the Auxiliaries just as they stopped a Crossley opposite his door. They dismounted and quickly came to the point.

'Did you see any Shinners today?'

'What!' said Liam.

'Any Shinners,' they repeated.

'What are Shinners?' asked Liam.

'Oh, Shinners, the IRA you know.'

'I don't know them either,' he said, 'but I saw soldiers passing.'

'Soldiers,' they said. 'No soldiers passed this way today.'

'Oh, but they did,' said Liam. 'They went up that way,' pointing with his stick to Rahoona.

'Were they some of our men?' they asked.

'They could be,' said Liam, 'but they were not dressed like ye.'

'How were they dressed? Had they helmets on them? What did they wear on their heads?'

'Nothing at all,' said Liam.

'How were they dressed?'

'They had overcoats on their shoulders and breeches like

them,' pointing to an Auxie's riding breeches, 'and they had brown boots and gaiters.'

'Ah!' they exclaimed, 'were there many of them?'

'About two hundred,' said Liam.

'What did they look like? What kind of men were they?'

'Oh, fine, strapping young men, only one old man with grey hair, and I had great pity for him.'

'Why?'

'He was carrying a very heavy gun. It must be one of those machine-guns. Indeed, I had no pity for any other one of them, whoever they were.'

The Auxies looked doubtfully at Liam's small yard and the narrow road. Then one asked, 'Can I turn my car here?'

'Begor, I always turn mine there anyway,' Liam replied.

Liam's car was one donkey-power.

15

A DRIVE TO CORK CITY

Early in March 1921, the column was located at Cúm Uí Chlumháin, Ballyvourney. Things had quietened down since Coolnacahera, and the days were very peaceful.

Then one evening I heard, 'Hugie, you're wanted. Mick, you're wanted.'

Hugie was Eugene O'Sullivan, our Lewis gunner, and Mick was myself, his assistant. The speaker was Dan Donovan (Sandow). Dan's eyes were bright and he was smiling. We knew something was afoot. We followed him into Twomeys', our headquarters.

Within, we found our brigadier, Seán O'Hegarty; my brother Pat, our commandant; Jim Grey, our driver; Seán Murray, our instructor; and Corney O'Sullivan, our engineer. Seán came to the point quickly. With him and with all his officers there was no formality. While the highest proficiency in military skill had been attained in the use of arms and by necessary exercises, yet formal salutations and the like were intolerable to him, and indeed to all concerned. Now he addressed us thus:

'Flurrie has found out that Strickland and a party will be going on a trip down the river from Cork the day after tomorrow. We'll try and sink them at the Marina. Dan will be in charge. Jim, of course, will drive the Buick. Seán and Corney are going, and Hugie and Mick with the Lewis. Ye will go to Donoughmore tonight by the old route. After the curfew patrols are withdrawn in the morning in the city, ye must get to the southern side of the river. Then stay tomorrow night at Ballygarvan. Mick Murphy will meet ye at Kaper Daly's pub, Farmers' Cross, on the following morning, and take ye in to the city. Be as careful as ye can.'

We got ready for our journey. The Buick tourer was a silent and powerful car that Jim maintained at its original efficiency. We had no fears on that score. Neither had anyone any fears as regards the driving. Jim himself always proclaimed that he was in mortal terror of coming events.

'Glory be to God, lads,' he would exclaim piously, 'I'm terribly windy.'

This was treated as a standard joke. Now we waited for it as the finale to our preparations.

The hood was lowered and strapped down. The top half of the windscreen was removed and a rectangular piece of plate glass was cut and removed from the corner of the lower half, remote from the driver. This was done to provide a convenient rest for the Lewis gun when facing forward. Tea was announced. We adjourned to the house. When it was over, night had fallen. Night was always our best ally. Without its aid, the weak could hardly hope to fight or resist the strong. Now under its friendly cover we were about to move nearer to the enemy. Fully armed, we took our places in the Buick. Most of the column stood around to wish us God speed, and I also suspect, to listen to Jim's valedictory.

He took his place at the wheel. Seán Murray sat next to him, then Hugie with his gun resting on the windscreen frame. In the back seat Corney sat immediately behind Jim, Sandow in the middle behind Seán. I sat behind Hugie. On the floor at my feet were the Lewis drums in their carriers. The car stood in the light from the house and with its own lights burning. Jim got out and walked around the Buick for a final inspection of tyres. Then he took his place again and, grasping the wheel, said with emphasis, 'Well, *in ainm an diabhal*, lads, I'm terribly windy!'

A mighty burst of laughter greeted the pronouncement, and in its heartening atmosphere the grey car slipped quietly away.

We travelled with dim lights as a rule. Only in certain valleys were the headlamps used, screened by the hills from enemy posts. At that time if you met a car on the road you could be certain it contained the enemy, for no other was allowed by them to travel. Thus, when we travelled and met people on the road, we passed as Black and Tans or Auxiliaries. We were in some danger from our own people. There was always the chance that some enterprising IRA man might, like Nelson, put his blind eye to the telescope and his good eye on us. Otherwise, it generally served us well to be taken for the enemy.

We passed quietly through Coolea and Ballyvourney, and for a short distance along the road to Macroom. Then by quiet roads through Liscarragane, where the great Canon O'Leary (An t-Ahair Peadar) was born. We passed the door where he stood, as a ragged little boy of eight, to watch and faithfully record the ghastly procession of the famine. Then, a few miles more, and we were at Carraig an Ime, where fell the gallant Art Ó Laoghaire fighting alone against the English. From Carraig an Ime through Ballinagree and Rylane to Donoughmore our journey was uneventful, but tiring on Jim, especially since lights had to be used sparingly.

At Donoughmore we were entertained by the 6th Battalion, and we rested until dawn. We had time to spare, since we had to wait until the curfew patrols and armoured cars were withdrawn at 7.30 a.m. We had breakfast, and we started off on the Donoughmore–Blarney–Cork road. For a time we enjoyed the long straight stretches where we could see well ahead of us. For there was the possibility of meeting with a strong raiding party of many lorries. That would be their time for such a job. Should they come, we would have time to stop and take up defensive positions. But, leaving the Blarney highway, we did not appreciate the lovely woodland road which changed direction so often. However, we met no enemy and reached St Ann's safely. On to the Kerry Pike where Seán stopped to see his mother. Estimating that our time would now be right, without a further stop, we dropped down to the Asylum Road. We got to the end without incident and crossed the bridge over the northern branch of the Lee. A run of a few hundred yards and we were moving at a smart pace down the Western Road.

Safety catches were 'off'. There was to be no delay in case of an attempt to interfere with us. Any enemy agents we met who took us for friends, we should give them the benefit of the mistake. We should hope to maintain that relation for some time. Although we were ready for instant action, and the Lewis and rifles were plain to be seen, yet we reclined apparently at ease as befitted Auxiliaries of the better-off class – not those fellows who sat stiffly on hard seats on Crossley tenders. We were now in Washington Street, and soon we could see to the end of it. We watched the junction with Main Street. All clear. What would the Grand Parade reveal? We swept gracefully into it in a right-hand quarter-circle, while our eyes instinctively swept from Patrick Street corner to the Mall, noting particularly Tuckey Street corner. Soon we were past that abode of a vile mixture, RIC and Black and Tans. Turning left, we were in the South Mall.

A few hundred yards, and we turned right over Parliament Bridge, across the south channel of the Lee.

Crossing the quay, we went up Barrack Street and past Cat Fort gate, where a Black and Tan sentry stood with sloped rifle. He brought his right hand across to the small of the butt, then down smartly to his side. A salute. The first half of it looked bad. Good manners carry one a long way. A few of us returned it wearily.

Some little time after passing by Cat Fort, we overran our road to the left. There was some doubt as to where the next road to the left led. We decided to enquire. This proved to be more troublesome than we expected. We could see people approaching us as if hurrying to work, yet they never reached us. They turned in a doorway or a gateway or a street. When we rushed to the corner of the street to shout after them, they had vanished. We felt that we were not popular. At length we chased a young man going in our own direction, and grabbed him as he turned in a wicket-gate. He was frightened, but would tell us nothing. Then Corney asked him, 'Would you not like to do something for Ireland?'

His eyes travelled over us all before he answered. We were amused at his confusion, and our smiles reassured him. 'I would,' he answered boldly.

He stood on the running-board, and, having piloted us around a few corners, brought us out on the road we wanted.

'God bless ye boys,' he exclaimed fervently as we parted.

In a short time we reached Miss Walsh's of Ballygarvan, where we were most hospitably entertained. We rested until the time for our appointment with Mick Murphy. We met him and Tadhg Sullivan at Kaper Daly's. Tadhg was introduced to us by Mick as 'the Republican Jewman'. A splendid-looking man, with laughing eyes, he had certainly a Semitic expression. They had no good news for us. Strickland was to attend the funeral of General Cummins who had been killed at Clonbanin and we were destined, therefore, not to meet him. Mick and Tadhg returned to the city. We were to meet Mick again, but it was our last meeting with Tadhg. Within a few days we heard with the greatest sorrow of his death in an encounter with a raiding party.

Jim wanted tyres for the Buick. It was settled that he and I should go to the city in the morning to get the tyres, some three-in-one oil and a few other messages. We met a reliable man that night who agreed to take us in his milk cart. We started early, seated facing forward and surrounded by churns. We wore our trench coats and gaiters, a very foolish thing to do, since it invited attention. In the milk cart it looked the part well enough, but when we went shopping–

'You might have shaved yourself at least,' I remonstrated with Jim. 'Even if you had shaved a week ago,' I added.

'You're wrong,' said Jim. 'I will pass as a benevolent old toff. It is you whom they will be after. Let me quote the *Hue and Cry* for you: "Wanted – Clean-shaven youth – Blue eyes

– Fair hair – Tall – Fanatical appearance. Dangerous young criminal."'

'Wait a bit,' I said. 'Wanted – Young man – Hardened appearance – Blue eyes – Fair hair – Tall – Desperate character – Unshaven – Forgot razor at scene of last murder.'

So we joked until we parted with our milk cart not far from the City Hall.

We walked over Parnell Bridge and turned left along the South Mall. As we crossed the street from the Mall to the South Gate Bridge I thought of yesterday morning, when we passed over the same ground with our four comrades in the Buick, the Lewis, our rifles and grenades. Now we were sadly reduced in numbers, our good car and armaments lacking. Besides, our position was further weakened by our attire. It cried out for attention from the enemy. We had not met them yet. We had not long to wait.

We crossed from the southern side of the Mall to the eastern side of the Parade. This we did to avoid Tuckey Street corner. In any case it was a near way. No sooner were we on the footpath than we saw a Rolls Royce Whippet armoured car bearing down on us on our side. Jim reacted immediately.

'Monkey Mac the spotter is in that car,' he said, 'and he knows me as well as a bad halfpenny. We'll cross.'

We crossed the first half of the wide Parade. The car was cruising along slowly, a sign that there was a spotter aboard.

We had to chance Tuckey Street or the car. We chose Tuckey Street, but there were twenty Black and Tans at the corner and it was out of the frying pan into the fire.

There was a middle course at first but it ran out on us. People were walking in the middle of the street towards the Fountain. We went with them. They screened us for a time from both the car and the crowd at the corner. Then they got a notion, all together, like geese, and made a drive towards the car, leaving us a target for the eyes of the Black and Tans. Those fellows had nothing else in life to do now but to watch us. Without speaking we both veered towards them. There was nothing else to be done.

We approached them slant-wise as if hitting for Tuckey Street. Undoubtedly, it was the best policy and we could hope to get away with it were it not for our appearance. We passed in front of them and about ten yards away from them. They said not a word until we were ten yards past them. Every man of them was engaged in assessing us during our march past. Each said to himself, 'That's the IRA uniform. But why the devil should they march so brazenly towards us and parade in front of us? Better see all the same.' They did.

There was some conversation, during which we gained a further ten yards. Then, 'Halt!'

We did not stop. The 'halt' was repeated, and we heard footsteps running behind us. We stopped and looked back. A Black and Tan came running towards us. We walked slowly back to meet him. Jim was the nearer to him and I lagged behind. Now he stood in front of Jim with his hands outstretched and raised slightly, in the attitude of one preparing to search.

'What is your name?' he asked Jim.

'Grey,' Jim replied.

'Grey! From where?'

'Cork Barracks,' said Jim.

Jim took a chance. His name was mud at Cork Barracks for some time, but the Black and Tan at Tuckey Street did not know. It impressed him undoubtedly. Now there was another diversion. A sudden gust of wind blew off his peaked cap, and it rolled along the ground towards me. Stooping, I caught it, straightened up and, walking towards him with a pleasant smile, gave it to him. He was delighted. It was not often that a Black and Tan received such courtesy.

'Thank you very much indeed,' he said with a smile. 'I suppose you have not a gun on you,' he added, as raising his hands high he brought them down in a slow sweeping motion, the motion of searching or feeling for a hidden weapon. This movement of the hands was merely a show for his comrades at the corner. He never touched my body. Neither did he touch Jim's. I must say he was a decent-looking man for a Black and Tan. His face showed no signs of the brutality that stamped most of them as a type. I would have been sorry for him had he rubbed us the wrong way, for we had guns on us. Our lives were forfeit anyway this long time, and while, with our hands in the dog's mouth we were willing to try out diplomacy to its fullest extent, no enemy, however strong numerically, was going to deprive us of loaded guns and then torture and kill us at their leisure. Well over forty years have passed since that incident and it is still fresh in my memory. Indeed, while I have Jim Grey to revive it, there is no fear that I shall forget it. For when we meet and there is a quorum Jim does not fail to turn the laugh against me.

'Wisha, Mick,' he says, 'do you remember the day you picked up the cap for the Black and Tan in the Grand Parade?'

We left the Grand Parade and soon stood at the counter of Wallaces' shop in St Augustine Street. Scarcely had we done so, when Sheila and Nora came in with the news that the whole block of buildings around us was cordoned off and a search was proceeding. We looked out. Both ends of the narrow street were held. We slipped unnoticed across to St Augustine's Church. We went through the church to the Washington Street door. Washington Street was cordoned at the Parade and Main Street. We would have to wait and see. We knelt down and prayed while we waited. When we looked out they had gone. We returned to Wallaces' and got any news that was going from Sheila and Nora. Then I insisted on Jim going into a barber's shop at the corner for a shave. He did so and we started for Johnson and Perrotts garage to get the tyres. Jim was to go first, I twenty yards behind. Scarcely had we started when I noticed a man in civilian clothes fall in behind Jim and follow at a distance of ten yards. I fell in behind the tout at about the same distance. Jim turned many a corner and crossed many roads before we reached the open space in front of the garage. Then he crossed the open space and entered through the big door. The shadow followed to the big door but stopped at the doorway on the right-hand side. Hidden from view from inside, he craned his neck around the sliding door to watch Jim cross diagonally a space of floor to the office.

I had been an interested spectator from across the street. Satisfied, now that he had located Jim in the office, the tout took a pace backwards and had started to execute a left turn when my left hand fell on his neck. He struggled to complete the turn but failed. I pushed him in the doorway, and into the corner formed by the sliding door and its pillar. He demanded an explanation, but I asked him to wait for a little while. Presently Jim returned from the office.

'We will go, Mick,' he said. Then he caught sight of the prisoner. 'Who is he?' he asked.

'I don't know,' I answered and told him the story.

The man admitted that I had told the truth, that he had followed Jim, but said he had done so through idle curiosity.

'You were going to Union Quay,' Jim said gently, 'and now my poor man,' he added, 'you may carry on, but you'll never reach the place.' He made further protests against the idea that he meant to do us any harm and so we left him. We reported the matter to Flurrie. He was picked up, tried and acquitted. His plea was still that of idle curiosity. It seemed an extraordinary one, but all his people were found to be honest and in no way hostile towards us. We were glad to hear that he got the benefit of the doubt. To hear of a young Irishman convicted of spying on his own people would be the most melancholy news of all.

We finished our shopping and returned to our milk cart. The tyres had arrived and we stowed them under the seat and churns. Sitting aboard, we started out the Douglas Road. We had not gone far when we found the street partly blocked and a group of RIC searching every vehicle that passed either way. Driving up to the barricade we were motioned through without question. Evidently they tired of questioning the milkman who passed them by every day. In any case, since the advent of the Black and Tans, the RIC had ceased to be enthusiastic about the 'Law'. Very soon we were clear of the city and saw with relief the open country. It was good to be safely back at Ballygarvan with our four comrades and to see the Buick and the Lewis and our rifles again.

That night, having said goodbye to our kindly hostess, Miss Walsh, we started on our journey home to Ballyvourney. This time we chose the southern route, through

Ballinhassig, where we slipped by the rear of the barracks. They heard the Buick climbing the hill, however, and sent out a message to warn all posts that we had passed. Our road from the south led us to within a mile of the military barracks of Ballincollig and, since we could not use lights, we had to travel very slowly. Bypassing trenched roads delayed us further. Finally, we crossed the Lee at Rooves Bridge and came into Coachford as day was breaking. From Coachford we went north to Peake, thence north-west to Ballinagree. Here we rested during the day as we got word that the Auxies were out across our road home. When night fell we returned by our old route to Carraig an Ime and reached our camp at Cúm Uí Chlumháin before midnight. Approaching, with full lights on, a narrow part of the road shaded by trees, a horse cart was suddenly run in front of us, bringing us to a stop. Around us we could see muzzles of rifles and shotguns, but nothing else.

'All right lads,' shouted Jim.

It was the guard for the night. They welcomed us home.

16

KNOCKSAHARING

Knocksaharing, literally translated into English, means 'Saturday Hill'. But it is probably the hill dedicated to Saturn. On top of the hill is a big rock known as Carraig a' tSagairt, where Mass was said in the penal days, but which in Druidical times was possibly a pagan altar.

The northern slope of Knocksaharing comes down to meet the southern slope of Clohina. In the depression so formed flows the little river, the Sullane Beag, and parallel to it runs the Macroom–Renanirree road. It was a lovely glen at the time I write about, with its clumps of holly everywhere, surrounding the little green fields and mingling with the stunted oak to form Clohina wood. As quiet a spot as one who longed for peace could wish to meet. The cascading of the little river, down the slope to the bridge at Átha Tiompáin, was a sound which spoke everlastingly of rest. The little bridge was but half a mile north of the place where I was born. To me it was once the bridge of romance, a goal

I longed to reach. I pictured it a mighty structure spanning a wide and deep current. When I managed to walk to it and was held on its parapets, to gaze on the rippling water underneath, I was quite pleased with it and I never wearied of that pleasure, even when later I discovered that it was but a very small bridge after all. The road it carried was the nearest way to Ballyvourney from the village of Kilnamartyra. It was much used by us at this time. It was quiet and the enemy made little use of it, deterred perhaps by the frowning Rahoona and its foothills, where marksmen might lie close to the road in safety.

It was the eve of the Feast of Corpus Christi 1921. The column had been disbanded for the time being. A round-up was impending and it was thought wiser to disperse the men. It proved to be a wise decision, as, soon after, a wider area than was anticipated was literally trampled by ten thousand troops. Seven of us kept together. Corney O'Sullivan, Jim and Miah Grey, Paddy Donncha Eoin, Patsy Lynch, my brother Pat and I. Six were armed with rifles and revolvers, while I carried the light aeroplane Lewis gun. We had come at nightfall to the house of our good friend Patsy Dinneen at Lios Buí Beag, a mile south-west of Kilnamartyra Cross. We never went early to bed in Patsy's farmhouse. He himself, his wife and family were all active comrades of ours, from the start to the finish of our campaign. Here was always the genuine and generous welcome. The possible consequences of our coming were not thought of. They never counted what might be the cost of harbouring us. They did not look forward to the chances of our being trapped in their home by the enemy. If we succeeded in breaking through and getting away, they would still have had to suffer heavily. Their entire property would be destroyed and possibly their menfolk shot or at least thrown into prison. But they never thought of that and when we reminded them of it they gave it scant consideration. Patsy used to say, 'It would be no harm to stir up things around here, the place is very quiet anyway.'

Nevertheless, we always felt we were doing wrong when we rested at such a homestead, without posting at least one sentry. At that time, there were area signal stations by night and by day. Beacons on hilltops were lighted at night when the enemy was observed leaving his base. These beacons were relayed forward and proved of great value on several occasions when the enemy ventured out on a raid.

I remember Saint John's night when the enemy was signalled by our beacons. At the same time, fires were lighted in honour of Saint John. This caused dire confusion and some slight strain in relations between the patrons of Saint John and the disciples of Baal. The latter decreed, like King Laoghaire, that in future, 'till Baal's enkindled fire shall rise, no fire shall flame instead'. Perhaps the enemy thought to avail of the confusion, but in any case he had not come very far when he changed his mind and returned again.

It was the morning of the Feast of Corpus Christi. We were sound asleep when we got the news. It was Mrs Dinneen herself who urgently called us: 'The Black and Tans, lads, the Black and Tans,' she cried. I ran to an upstairs window, and looked out. They were not yet in sight at any rate.

Just then Jer, her son, appeared and shouted, 'No hurry, no hurry!' He had come from early Mass. While we dressed, he told us the news.

'They crossed Carrigaphooca bridge,' he said, 'and we waited to see if they would go straight on for Ballyvourney. But no, they came on for the Cross (our village), and crossing Con Lynch's bridge went on by the lower road to Renanirree. So there ye are.'

There we were as Jer said, trying hard to anticipate their further movements. We asked each other what they were likely to do next. While hurriedly drinking a cup of tea, we pondered on it. They were a strong party, seven lorries of Auxiliaries, and they might do anything. They were not at all shy of travelling over byroads. In fact, it had become popular with them, as it contributed towards their safety. The main roads had become dangerous for them, so when they chose a quiet route the chances were much in their favour. Returning by a different and circuitous way was another favourite manoeuvre of theirs, and had often saved them from unwelcome attention. It was impossible to watch for them on more than one road at the same time, since we had not the armed numbers to do so. We could not block a large percentage of all the roads, since we would greatly harm our own people. Where roads had been trenched, a rough bypass had been allowed for the use of horse traffic. The year 1921 had an unusually fine, dry summer and the motor transport of the enemy often got through the bypasses easily, or crossed trenches over specially made planks. So the game of hide-and-seek went on and we were now at our wits' end to forecast the Auxiliaries' movements on reaching Renanirree. They could go on through the glen to Ballingeary. They could turn north to Ballyvourney. They could go south over Doiranaonaig to Inchigeela, or go along the Toon road a mile to the south of us and so return to Macroom. Or they could come from the Toon road past our gate and go home by the Cross. Or they could come by the upper road from Renanirree to the Cross, and pass within half a mile of us at Bearnasalach. And having come to Bearnasalach they could even say, 'There's the road to Patsy Dinneen's. He'll be terribly distressed if he hears we passed and never called.'

Three or four of us must have thought of the solution together. There was a sudden upsurge of men, which nearly wrecked the table. For a moment a babel of short questions and shorter answers.

'Sinn Féin court!' 'Bloody judges!' 'Captured documents!' 'The bag!' 'Renanirree!' And the seven of us were streaking out of the door, through the haggard gateway, over a fence and making a beeline for Knocksaharing. A few days before we had heard of the capture, by the enemy, of a bag containing some documents. It was said to belong to a judge who was on a circuit of Sinn Féin courts. In the bag was a reference to the court which was to have been held at Renanirree on that very day. Needless to say, it was not now being held. But now we had a reasonable clue to the movements of the Auxies. They had gone to see if the court was being held at the appointed time. They would not delay there and since it was not a routine visit there would be no danger in returning by the same road.

Our time was short. To intercept them at the nearest point we would have to travel two miles over hedges and ditches. Renanirree was but three miles from that point. My uncle's house was straight across our path and we found him, with two other local Volunteers, lying in the sun on Carraig a' Radhairc. They produced two service rifles from a dump and the three of them accompanied us. My uncle's house stood a hundred yards south of the upper Renanirree road. We crossed this with some little caution and went swiftly upwards to the ridge of Knocksaharing, passing by the Mass rock of Carraig a' tSagairt. Then we quickly descended the northern slope, through small fields of every shape with their big stone fences, which generations had made at a terrible cost of murderous toil. Soon we reached the spot we sought, a corner of one of these little fields. It sloped steeply towards the lower Renanirree road. A bad corner to get out of, if one had to. But it commanded a long stretch of the road to Macroom and was back from it only thirty yards. We had not a long view of the oncoming enemy. This was one of our fears. If some of the rear lorries stopped to the west of us, the Auxies could work up an easy gradient and come down on us in the pocket we were in. We could not see them at this manoeuvre, so we decided to send the two local Volunteers across the road into Clohina wood. My uncle went with them. They crossed the river by the little plank bridge and soon signalled to us from an excellent position in the wood. We had not long to wait. One of the two riflemen returned with a suggestion that their position would be a good one for the Lewis gun. I told him that since we had little hope of stopping the lorries, I was going to follow them down the road with a raking fire and that I had command of all the four hundred yards to Átha Tiompáin. He agreed that I was in a better position and had mounted the fence to leave when I dragged him down again. The first lorry was almost on the firing line. The chagrin of the rifleman was terrible. He made a movement as if to dash down the steep slope to the road. He had left his rifle at the other side. I tried to console him.

'It will be all right,' I said, 'Dan will take care of it.'

As if in answer, a rifle loudly spoke from Clohina wood. I

opened fire into a steel-plated lorry. The men sat on its floor around the sides, their legs extended inwards. It passed from my sight for the time being, and I turned my attention to the next. I favoured each with a burst of fire, and quickly changed the drum for a full one. Six lorries were now speeding down the road to Átha Tiompáin. I enfiladed them generally. The rifles near me were still firing at right angles to the road. Soon the six lorries, three tenders and three plated Crossleys passed from my sight just beyond the crossroads. The seventh and last tender had stopped just underneath us. It was quite close, too close to sight it even, for it had been ditched under the lee of a high bank. We could not locate a single one of its occupants, but some of them appeared to be very active, for they maintained a heavy fire. The two riflemen in the wood could not see them because of a thick hedge on their side of the road. The Auxies could not cross the road to fire through the hedge because of us, but they tried another method. Crouching under the bank on our side, they fired rifle grenades over the hedge. These fell in the wood and exploded with a lot of noise, but did no harm. We had brought no hand grenades with us and now regretted it. For a few grenades dropped over the bank would have routed out the Auxies onto the road again. It would have been madness to cross the fence and run down the steep slope to fire down on them, so the only method left was to send a few to take them from the Renanirree side if possible.

A shout from Caherdaha hill drew our attention to the east. A man stood on a fence and pointed downwards to Átha Tiompáin. After the first outburst of firing, and as we had watched the lorries disappear down the road to Macroom, we had heard a wild cheer from the same point. A group that watched there had given vent to their feelings in a *Gáir Chatha*. The group was still there, but now they had sounded a warning. The lorries had stopped just out of our sight and now the Auxies were coming back in skirmishing order along the high ground on both sides of the road. There was no hurry, but yet any delay might endanger us. We had a wholesome respect for the activity and physical fitness of the Auxies, if they found out that only a small group was opposed to them. Woe to the man or men who allowed them to get the impression that they were weak in any way, for then they followed up relentlessly. In our case they had not yet caught sight of us and so they would move cautiously. They already had experience of our heavy fire and I have no doubt, were it not for the ditching of their lorry, they would not have returned at all. But they could not return to Macroom and admit that they had left their comrades to fight it out alone. So they must return to find them and, since we had not a few more men to keep in touch with their flanks, we must withdraw. Sending the unarmed Volunteer by a detour to the west to withdraw my uncle and his comrade, we also moved westwards to meet them and again crossed the ridge of Knocksaharing and the upper Renanirree road. Leaving my uncle's house we went southwards to Lios Buí, where an aeroplane hovered over us in an azure sky. It circled about as if looking for a movement of troops. That was one decided advantage we had over the enemy; we could, without aeroplanes, easily discover troop movements, while it was quite impossible for them to detect ours, for the simple reason that the troops did not exist. It would require keen eyes to see the seven of us reclining against a rock in the middle of the Lios Buí bogs.

The day being still young, and we feeling hungry, we crossed the Toon river to the Claonrath houses where we had tea. Then, as the sun started to decline, we retraced our steps to Patsy Dinneen's where we heard the news of the day. The Auxiliaries had retrieved their comrades and the lorry and started for Macroom. At Carrigaphooca, three miles from the town, they found the road blocked by trees. In a panic, they tore them away and broke through. Reaching Macroom, they found that the workhouse had been burned in their absence. It had not been, for them, a very profitable day. They had, in fact, received 'more kicks than ha'pence'.

We were unable to find out anything about the enemy's losses on that day. The Auxies reported that they had no casualties. They would do that in any case, but we could not claim that we had inflicted any, even if we had killed numbers of them in the lorries. We had not even the opportunity of seeing what happened to the one that was ditched. The one thing certain was that they had got a bad fright. They had come out to Renanirree expecting to find a number of people, unarmed, gathered together in the school or dance hall. Had they found them, they would, like the brutal yeoman Hempenstall, have constituted themselves as judge, jury, hangman, gallows, rope and all.

* * *

We rejoiced to hear of the destruction of the 'Union of Macroom', or the 'workhouse' or the 'poorhouse' as it was variously called. That cursed institution, and all the others of its kind throughout the country, had been for long the nightmare of the people. For too long they had obtruded their obscene presence between them and the light of God. What untold suffering of mind and body did their vile and ugly walls and gates encompass, not so long ago! But suffering and despair were not confined to their compass or environs. Their influence went abroad like a virulent miasma, like Cromwell's corpse 'to poison half mankind'. Built, ostensibly, as chari-table institutions, the devil quickly became their patron. Charity, the most formidable of virtues, was soon deleted from his programme. As an instrument of oppression, the poorhouse far surpassed the gaol or the hangman's rope. For it struck at the whole family. First, it haunted the parents. If the landlord wanted their land or they failed to pay the rent, what were their prospects? If they had the money they could emigrate. That would be bad enough. But failing that, only the poorhouse. The prospect of death would not appal an Irish man or woman unduly. But the poorhouse, where the father would be separated from the mother, and the brother from the sister – what torture could be more diabolically devised? Yet it happened in the poorhouse of Macroom, and Canon Peter O'Leary (An t-Ahair Peadar) has given the names of the family and the details of their sufferings in *Mo Sgéal Féin*. He tells how Diarmaidín was separated from Sheila, his little sister, how he died and his body was thrown into the pit at Carraig a' Staighre with other Famine victims; how Sheila soon followed him there; and how, a few days later, the father and mother struggled home to die.

He records how Pádraig and Cáit stopped at the pit at Carraig a' Staighre. Somewhere underneath were the bodies of their children. But their bright souls were in a better world, 'where tyrants taint not nature's bliss'. Having cried enough, they turned their faces towards their cabin in Doire Lia, six miles away to the north-west. Here they were found the following morning by a neighbour, both dead. Cáit's feet were clasped by Pádraig to his breast inside his shirt. It had been his last effort to save her life.

Canon O'Leary almost lived to see the poorhouse laid low. How the man who wrote *Mo Sgéal Féin* would rejoice with us at its passing!

17

THE BIG ROUND-UP

The big round-up started on the evening of Sunday 5 June 1921 at Ballyvourney. We had been expecting it daily for at least a fortnight and the column had been disbanded in the face of it. Seven of us had so far kept together, Corney O'Sullivan, Jim and Miah Grey, Paddy Donncha Eoin, Patsy Lynch, my brother Pat and I. We had stayed in the neighbourhood of the village or Cross of Kilnamartyra, at Lios Buí, or Kilmacarogue, or Doirín na Ceárdchan, or Knocksaharing with our good friends and comrades. Now, on Saturday morning, we had got definite news that the round-up was about to begin on the morrow. In the kitchen of the old house at Knocksaharing we discussed the matter. My uncle was present with the seven of us.

While nothing very definite was known about the impending enemy operation, we knew that it was going to be very thorough and widespread. To anticipate its boundaries was now the vital consideration. Hitherto, when hard pressed, we had always crossed the border into Kerry, and when things had quietened down again had returned. Sure enough, there were large areas in Kerry that would escape encirclement in this round-up, but to select those areas was the crux. Again, it was obvious that the nearest safe part of Kerry during this period would be many miles from the Cork border. The weather was unusually fine and dry, and the mountains along and across the border would be well searched by enemy infantry. It was easy enough to search the same mountains. Most of them were bare and devoid of even heather. Certainly, a column of men could not hope to escape attention from enemy columns scattered about on the neighbouring hills. Even one man could not move without being seen by any fairly vigilant and well-posted sentry.

All of us present well knew the disadvantages of the bare Kerry mountain in a round-up or in a clash with stronger enemy forces. Yet, six voted to go to Kerry well beyond the western limit of the circle. To escape the net was not entirely their motive. Corney wanted to avail of the period of inactivity to pay a visit home to west Cork, and the others declared that they would accompany him some distance and then go further into Kerry to meet some of the Kerry men we knew. My uncle and I opposed the decision to go into any mountain country or to leave our own ground at all.

'I think,' said Dan, 'it is a great mistake to go near those mountains now, for they will be swarming with troops. I'd much prefer to keep the low, broken, boggy ground, be damned!'

The man was wise and the next few days were to prove his wisdom. However, the others decided to go and asked me to come with them. Reluctantly, I agreed and the seven of us left together. We had travelled over half a mile across country towards Renanirree when I stopped and asked the others again to consider staying where we were, or even to go in the opposite direction. I told them that they were going to be chased if not caught on the bare mountains and that they would have a peaceful week anywhere to the south or east of us. It was no use. I wished them luck and watched them go, for I felt lonely when they left me. I would have gone with them against my own judgment, but I had another reason for staying as well.

I returned to Knocksaharing, and that night my uncle and I slept peacefully at Patsy Cooney's of Kilmacarogue, a quarter-mile from Dan's home. All the following afternoon and until late in the evening, I lay stretched in the heather on top of one of the foothills of Rahoona. It commanded an excellent view of the winding Ballyvourney road at Poul na Bró, and stretches here and there as far east as Coolavokig. Equipped with a powerful pair of field glasses, little could pass unknown to me.

One did not need glasses to see the enemy, however. About two o'clock the procession started. The massed columns of infantry formed its principal feature. It was an imposing display, calculated to overawe as well as to destroy. The infantry was made up of most of the regular troops from Cork and Ballincollig barracks. Their motor transport, with tents, field kitchens and other impedimenta added to the display. Besides these regulars and their gear, the Auxiliaries with their Crossleys gave me the impression that, apart from the cat, very few had been left to mind the house. Having seen this methodical and massive movement of military force, from east to west, I was left in no doubt about its objective. It would be some point beyond the village of Ballyvourney, to the west or north of it. In fact it proved to be the valley of Claodach at the foot of the Paps mountains.

The valley of Claodach is a deep pocket between the hills, four miles to the north-west of Ballyvourney. From a military point of view it was a veritable cul-de-sac. Only one long winding road led into it from the west at that time. This would, in the ordinary way, have been an advantage, since enemy lorries could not converge on the glen. But the incursion of infantry from all sides was made feasible by the unusually fine weather. So, early on Monday morning, a ring of steel was closed around Claodach. Ten thousand men made up that circle which, as the day wore on, gradually contracted. It was a real day out for the British, a day on the moors. Every man, old or young, was shot at on sight. An old man at the county border, near the Killarney road, was gazing upwards at an aeroplane when a volley was fired at him. A bullet grazed his throat, but missed the vital arteries. The poor harmless old man never dreamt that the 'sportsmen' were out for Irish blood that day. From early morning until late afternoon the firing went on. Two young men were killed early in the day on a hilltop north of the Claodach valley. Evidently they had moved away from the northern contracting arc, expecting to find safety somewhere to the south. Like grouse or other game, however, they were flushed out of their native heather to provide targets for the British warriors. They killed them and disputed among themselves as to who were the successful marksmen. Their shooting would, no doubt, have been far less accurate had the poor lads had any kind of a firearm with which to return even an occasional shot.

It was said at the time that the enemy forces, ten thousand in number, had converged on the Claodach valley to encircle and destroy an IRA army of one thousand men. Now there was no such thing, even scattered over the whole of Munster. The odds against a thousand men would have been ten to one, had such an army existed. On Monday morning, the enemy, moving from every point of the compass on Claodach, interviewed every person they met. They had the same story for everyone. A thousand IRA men were waiting for them in Claodach. Had the enemy been really certain of this they would not have advanced with such confidence. Fifty men was about the number they expected to take in. That would provide them with ample sport for the day. But twenty times fifty? What a pity such a force could not have been waiting for them. But, could it have been mustered, it would not have been waiting in Claodach for Monday morning to dawn. It would have been down on Sunday afternoon to meet them on the Ballyvourney road. As I watched them march past on that evening I looked in vain for some flanking protection for the massed battalions, but there was none. They just marched stolidly through Coolnacahera and Poul na Bró. Had they dreamt that a thousand IRA men were assembled within six miles of them, their disposition would have been entirely different.

On Sunday afternoon, a local Volunteer, Murt (Twomey), left the village in good time before the influx of foreign troops to Ballyvourney. While walking uphill to the north, Murt decided that to keep on in that direction, or perhaps to the west or south, would end only in his capture a long way from home. He decided to return and, since there was little chance of his being identified as an IRA man, to pass off as a peaceful citizen. Reaching home, he called out his dogs, and walked away to the south as far as the bridge over the Sullane. Here he waited until he saw the advance troops enter the village. The road from the village turns eastwards after crossing the river on its southern side and about a hundred yards from the bridge stood Seán Jer's cottage. Seán was the father of one of our best Volunteers. Seán himself was at home, but none of his sons. As the soldiers entered the village, about four hundred yards away, a few people were on the road near Seán's cottage. One of them was a visitor to the district. Instead of walking away to the east along the road, sheltered by a good fence, he leaped over the southern fence and ran straight up the high fields of the Curragh hill in view of the soldiers. A heavy fire was immediately directed at him. He escaped, but Seán Jer coming out to drive his cow to safety was himself mortally wounded. Murt, under cover of the road fence, managed to reach the cottage and dash in under fire. The fire was maintained and a stream of bullets passed through the open door. Presently an officer with a party arrived. Murt persuaded them to help him bring Seán indoors and lay him in a comfortable position, as he was suffering terrible pain. Then, after further parley, they allowed him to go in search of a priest and a doctor. Murt returned to the village after a fruitless quest and was challenged by some Auxiliaries who were present in great strength.

'What are you doing to and fro here for some time?' they demanded.

'I am looking for a priest and doctor for a man who was shot over there,' Murt replied.

'Who shot him?' they said.

'It must have been some of your men,' said Murt.

'Can you prove that?' they again demanded threateningly, as they gathered around him.

Murt wisely compromised by saying that he could not, but that he was sent by a military officer on his mission. On hearing this they let him go. Meeting with an officer, who again questioned him, Murt asked him for the service of a military doctor. The officer directed him to the Red Cross station where he found a doctor who agreed to attend to Seán.

On the following morning Murt went to see Seán again. He was now taken by a party of soldiers and, with a few other local men, ordered to help at the erection of bell tents on the inch near the bridge. Murt made a bad start. A mallet was handed to him and he was directed to drive some pegs. Aiming a vicious blow at one, the head of the mallet flew off and struck the sergeant on the head. Mad with rage and pain, he snatched up a rifle and Murt thought his end had come. The sergeant cooled off, however, and he and others contented themselves with telling Murt and his companions of the fun they would have in the evening when the column was brought in. Murt listened patiently. Presently, when that party had finished their erections, they allowed him to go his own way again. As he left the field he saw a clip of ammunition on the ground. This he surreptitiously transferred to his pocket and went towards home. A few hundred yards ahead of him at the village cross he saw a sentry. Dropping the clip of cartridges into a convenient hole in the stone fence, he carried on. At the cross he was halted by the sentry and all his pockets were carefully searched. Soon, however, they got to know him and did not further molest him. Indeed, some of the Tommies were anxious to open trade relations with him. One of them offered a fine pair of officer's leggings for three shillings. Murt said he had no money about him. Credit was forthcoming, however, the gaiters were handed over and an appointment was made for the transfer of the hard cash. Each kept the appointment at a different rendezvous. Soon after, the Tommy shocked and astonished some of the villagers as he went about inquiring for 'that —— Murt who had kept his three shillings'. Later on Murt found him and the matter was amicably settled.

Late on Sunday evening I located the main camp of the enemy. It was situated very favourably relative to the Curragh hill, I thought, as I went home in the twilight. I knew the ground well. It would be easy, in the semi-darkness of the June night, to come down the western slope of Rahoona, slip across the Dubh-Glaise river and the road at Cathair Ceárnach, and, moving cautiously upwards over the eastern scrubby shoulder of the Curragh, approach to within four hundred yards of the huge growth of bell tents. I might not succeed in doing much material damage, I reflected, but at least I would stir up the big hornet's nest. Moreover, having spent a tough and unprofitable day in Kerry, the insult to the mighty war machine would be keenly felt by its patrons. I slept soundly at Kilmacarogue until late in the morning.

Towards evening I came to Knocksaharing and started to equip myself for the rough four miles across country. First, I got ready the light aeroplane Lewis gun. Next I put on a strong military haversack and one by one stowed into it the spare Lewis drums. I felt I could carry five, although my total load, including a Mauser pistol, was heavy. Having securely fastened all my gear, I shouldered my gun and set off in the gathering dusk.

I kept to the fields from the very start, intending to cross roads only in favourable places and at right angles. The reason for this caution was that I had heard that two more military camps had been established not far away to the south-west and west. I even avoided the road from my uncle's gate to the boreen leading to Gurtanedin. The spot where I chose to cross the road was a most lonely and unfrequented place. I stepped out from behind a rock, crossed the road and dropped on one knee in a shallow depression just on the roadside. There was no fence to the road and just in front of me I heard voices. Presently there was a stumbling of many feet down a steep slope ten yards away from me. Clumps of rushes grew on either side of me. In fact I was in the middle of a *lochán*, now dried up by the prolonged fine weather. I had hoped that the oncoming group would make a detour of the *lochán*, which had a fairly steep bank five or six feet in front of me. But no. They did not see it at all. They stepped off into space and, half falling, half rising, passed on either side, narrowly escaping a collision with me. The jolt they got naturally loosened their tongues again and I knew by their accents that they were not of the enemy. Curiosity got the better of me.

'Where the devil are ye going to?' I asked.

I thought at the same time that perhaps the enemy was not far behind them. The voice immediately behind them caused the utmost confusion amongst them. I stood up and interviewed them. I knew most of them. They were not Volunteers, but would help as best they could. They had come from the Ballyvourney district to avoid being rounded up. I asked them where they proposed going to avoid the round-up.

'To Doiranaonaig,' they replied.

'There is a camp at Doiranaonaig,' I told them.

I pointed out the great danger of travelling together in a group. They had come down on to the road talking loudly and had the enemy been in my place they would have been greeted with a volley. Questions would be deferred until too late. There were many other reasons why they should not have left home at all. I had pity for them travelling thus, a target for the enemy. I asked them if they knew any friends to the south-east. One of the group had relations a few miles away in that direction, so it was decided to go to that place. Before leaving, they told me the news of the day from Ballyvourney. A number of prisoners had been brought in, among them a few members of the column. This was most depressing to hear and I could scarcely refrain from telling the bearers of the tidings how much everybody, including themselves, would benefit by their staying at home. However, I said nothing, but long after they had left I sat among the rushes trying to decide on what I ought to do. Until I had heard of the prisoners taken, I had been very happy about the project. I could have got one or more of my comrades to accompany me willingly, but would not think of risking anybody's life on such a scheme. Now I was confronted with the same responsibility. I argued the consequences with myself. Finally, I had to admit to the voice of reason, that, as a reprisal, the death of the prisoners would follow the shooting-up of the camp. In a very vicious humour I shouldered my gun and marched down the road to my uncle's gate. I had kept to the byways to avoid meeting people and, lo, they had nearly trampled me as they came laden with bad news.

My comrades who went to Kerry were, early on Monday, hard-pressed to avoid capture. Actually, they were within the circle which had, at dawn, started to join its various arcs. Moving quickly towards the oncoming enemy, they slipped through a gap which soon closed behind them. Other members of the column did likewise, in other directions. Some who had gone to Kerry had, on Sunday night, returned to the east of Ballyvourney. Thus, on Monday evening when the net was drawn, the enemy had little in it. Among a large number of prisoners assembled at Ballyvourney National School, they had two members of the column and a few other Volunteers. The military from Tralee, who took part in the round-up, carried with them two Volunteers. On the following day they released them, having failed to identify them.

Among the prisoners in the school at Ballyvourney were the two brothers Cronin, from Toureen, across the border in Kerry. Both were Volunteers and their home, like the neighbouring houses of Muing, was always our refuge when we needed a rest. Indeed, having once crossed their hospitable threshold, one found it hard to leave again. To sit by the fire, listening to the mother and her two sons discussing even very ordinary affairs, was a great joy in itself. A rich humour enveloped the most trivial matter. But when one of the three began to tell a story, we held our breath in gleeful anticipation. For the story-teller could assume the role of every character in the tale, merely by the change of facial expression and the inflexion of the voice. This natural talent was to prove of great value to them, and to others, while prisoners in the school on Monday evening.

A group of officers stood regarding the men they had hoped to classify as units of the IRA. If there were some among the officers who thought the 'bag' was good, there were others with a more discerning eye who thought otherwise. The matter was soon put to the test. An officer stepped forward and spoke to the prisoners: 'Here, you fellows, you will remain here for tonight; you may sleep there,' indicating the timber floor at large.

This announcement was not received with enthusiasm. There was no great rush to get to bed. Patsy Cronin slowly detached himself from his group. With a well-simulated slouch he crossed, in full view of the officers, to the farthest corner of the room. Here, stooping, he pressed the floor with the palms of both hands. Evidently not satisfied, he straightened himself a little and moved a few yards further along the wall. Again stooping, he tested the area of floor around him within the radius of his hands. With a frown he arose and, moving quickly forward, dropped down on his hands and knees to investigate again. An officer intervened.

'What the devil are you after?' he asked.

With a vacuous stare Patsy replied. 'I am looking for a soft board to lie on, sir,' he said.

Aghast at the revelation, it was now the officer's turn to stare. Then a smile of triumph flooded his features and, turning, he quickly walked back to his comrades.

'Did ye hear that?' he said. 'Now who was right? We have picked up all the imbeciles of the country!'

For that night, the prisoners had to be content with the bed that Patsy thought too hard. On the following day, they were, with one exception, all released. They were far from being imbeciles.

The man detained was a giant Volunteer, John J. Quill, from Bardincha, Coolea. He was taken by the Essex Regiment to Toames on Wednesday evening, en route for Kinsale. When captured, John became the target of jibes from the Tommies. They referred to him as 'Enormous Paddy', and wondered if he were as strong as he looked. At length, exasperated, John turned on them.

'I'd take any four of ye in the arse of my breeches for the whole day and never feel ye were there,' he told them.

They became quite respectful after that retort, and did not further annoy him.

The Essex Regiment or 'Percival's crowd' as they were called, were the last to leave Ballyvourney on Wednesday afternoon. I had been watching the exodus since the day before, from Rahoona hill, Candroma rocks and other vantage points overlooking the Ballyvourney road. All had, so far, returned by the way they had come, along that highway. I actually saw 'Percival's crowd' turn off the main road at Poul na Bró and come along by the foot of Rahoona. With plenty of time to spare, I reached Candroma rocks ahead of them. My intention was to catch them with enfilading fire from the Lewis gun as they ascended the long steep hill of Caherdaha. I would have given much for a shot at that murderous crowd. As they passed me by, I recognised John J. a prisoner among them. I was in no doubt about what the result for John would be if I fired on them. Some hours later, they wantonly fired at and killed Buckley at Toames. At the same time I must give the devil his due, and tell how one of Percival's party saved the life of my uncle before their rearguard had passed out of my sight. My uncle had come to the Cross for some provisions. His horse and cart were near the door of Den Buckley's shop and pub, which stood at the corner made by two roads. Down the hill from Caherdaha came the advance party on bicycles. Someone ran to the pub door and gave the alarm. Dan ran out, jumped on the car and went off at a fast trot. Reaching the corner, the cyclists saw him go. Dismounting, they unslung their rifles and shouted after him. He did not stop.

'Open fire on him,' several voices spoke together.

'No, do not,' said another, 'he does not hear you with the noise of the cart. I'll follow him.'

Mounting his bicycle, he chased and overtook the cart. My uncle pulled up, feigning surprise as well as he could.

'Did you not hear us call you,' the soldier asked.

'No,' my uncle lied, 'I heard nothing until you spoke.'

A few simple questions about his business at the village and where he was going to were put to him, and he was allowed to go.

The advance party now entered the pub. The day was warm and a dozen customers were on the premises. Nearly all were past military age and none could be accused of having a military appearance. Nevertheless, all were ordered out and lined up along the wall at right angles to the road. There they had to remain until the first of the main body arrived. Percival was on horseback and his attention was called to the prisoners. He did not leave his position to have a frontal view of them, but called a sergeant.

'Have a look at those,' he said.

The sergeant marched smartly to the end of the line remote from him. Starting his scrutiny he walked slowly back to the other end. Eyes front again he marched up to Percival. Saluting, he reported, 'There's not a Shinner amongst them, sir.'

Later on in the evening I came home to find my mother and Mrs Buckley, the wife of the owner of the pub, at our gate. Both were laughing heartily. Mrs Buckley had seen and heard the comedy from an upstairs window.

'"Not a Shinner amongst them," said he. And sure the man was right,' said Mrs Buckley to us. 'What were they, too, but a lot of little *dravelisheens.*'

I must explain that it was not at any lack of physical fitness that the people laughed, but that the group so contemptuously rejected by the sergeant had long before been rejected by the 'Shinners' as hostile but harmless.

18

THE CASTLE
OF MACROOM

The castle of Macroom stands on the banks of the Sullane, a few miles beyond the eastern boundary of our area. Yet it is relevant to speak of it, since it played a part, and not a helpful one, in the lives of our people. Again, Macroom was our nearest or home town.

The castle was first built by the O'Flynns in the twelfth century. Later it came into the possession of the Mac-Carthys. In 1602 it was besieged and damaged by Sir Charles Wilmot. This must have been its last stand as an Irish castle. It was burned down in 1641. Donogh Mac-Carthy restored it and the Papal Nuncio, Rinuccini, stayed in it for a short time in October 1645, while on his way from Kenmare to Kilkenny. Cromwell, in 1656, gave it to Admiral Sir William Penn. MacCarthy got it back on the Restoration. MacCarthy finally lost it in 1691.

The Hollow Sword Blade Company of London bought it by auction and sold it, at a profit of course, to Judge Bernard, ancestor of the Earls of Bandon. From the Bernards it was acquired by Robert Hedges Eyre. Eyre's daughter married Simon White of Bantry and their eldest son, Richard, was created Viscount Bantry in 1800 and Earl of Bantry in 1816. The third Earl modernised the castle and it passed on to his sister, Lady Ardilaun.

In 1920 it was taken over by the Auxiliaries. These were its last British occupants. In fairness to them, I must say that they were no worse than some of its former tenants.

Generally speaking, after the battle of Kinsale, the castle in Ireland became an instrument of slavery and repression. The seat of alien government was housed in Dublin Castle. The other castles through the country were occupied by Planters, or by people Irish in name perhaps, but no better than the Planters. Hugh O'Neill of Tyrone, brought up at an English court, well knew the value of the influence of the castle. Passing by Mourne Abbey on his way to the fatal field of Kinsale, he saw a castle on a hill.

'Who lives there?' he asked a local man.

'Oh, Barrett is his name,' answered the man. 'He is here a long time, nearly two hundred years, and he is a Catholic.'

'I hate the *bodach* as if he came only yesterday,' Hugh replied.

The Big House had a powerful denationalising effect on

the people. From time to time it pauperised, demoralised and tried to Anglicise them. The castle might be referred to as the great Big House. It co-ordinated the activities of all the Big Houses around it, as well as demoralising its own vicinity.

The main gateway to the castle of Macroom opens onto the square of the town. It is a feudal gateway, arched and battlemented. The main building stands back from it, just far enough for respectability and defence. A strong-walled, plain, rectangular, three-storeyed house, it had a flat roof with crenellated parapet. Its grounds extended for a mile along the River Sullane. A high wall, of course, enclosed them. The denizens of these places claimed to be exclusive in their ways and fastidious in their tastes. Yet, for years they managed to tolerate the sight of three heads impaled on the spikes on the highest point of the Bridewell, which overlooked the castle gates. But I think that Irish heads, artistically arranged, appealed to their aesthetic natures. Not until less than a hundred years ago was the practice discontinued. The people were themselves responsible for the lapse of this uplifting branch of the arts. They never appreciated it properly, even though it was, for them, part of a system of higher education.

I think there is nothing so melancholy to contemplate as a mental picture of those times that are past. The groups that stand on the square to watch the carriages and their escorts as they enter or leave the castle. Most of them came to get a glimpse of the lords and ladies and 'gentry', well-fed and well-dressed aliens. A few serfs actually doff their caps as they pass. The people have sunk to the lowest depth in the mire of slavery. But they are not yet altogether lost. Among them are a few who sigh deeply and turn away in sorrow and disgust. They belong to the 'Hidden Ireland', which is found everywhere, a fragment here and there even in the most unexpected places. Above the sordid scene, three heads stare disdainfully into space. They can see far and away beyond the range of the poor mortals who abridged their earthly vision. For now the road of time stretches interminably before them. A very short distance down that road they can see happening events that bring them joy. The flames of the castle and the poorhouse light their way for many a long and mortal year.

Even in the worst times, when all organised opposition to tyranny had been crushed, an individual arose and struck a blow for the motherland, 'to show that still she lives'. My father often told me of one of these warriors, a stout fellow known as Seán Rua an Ghaorthaig. True, he was known as an 'outlaw' or rapparee to the powers that were and to most 'respectable' people. In Irish history he would be classed with Redmond O'Hanlon and Eamon an Chnuic. In England he would be with Robin Hood or Locksley. History would be very poor stuff, in any country, without such men.

To the south of Macroom Castle, and immediately in front of it, Sléibhín hill rises green and fairly steep. Its other side, also green and steep, overlooks the Gaortha. The Gaortha is a low-lying area, a few square miles in extent, covered with brushwood, mostly alder, and water-logged by innumerable channels of the Lee. Here Seán Rua had retired from his enemies and for many years baffled all their attempts to dislodge him. He made his own powder for his firearms and it was said to be practically smokeless. He did not spend all his time hiding and inactive in the Gaortha. Now and again he sallied forth and exacted tribute from some Planter. Often did the 'gentry' muster against him with all the available local yeomanry or militia. But Seán always managed to elude them in the sheltering tangle of his natural fortress.

Seán Rua was a crack shot. Once, in disguise, he competed at a yeomanry musketry test in Macroom. A local sergeant, an expert shot, tied with him for the final. The unknown yeoman from a distant company beat the sergeant. Great was the chagrin when, too late, it was discovered that Seán Rua an Ghaorthaig had gone home with the prize. Seán had a high sense of humour and was prepared to run risks to gratify it.

A final and determined effort to eliminate Seán was decided on. Starting at the dawn of a mid-summer day all the 'gentry' and militia surrounded the Gaortha. Gradually and thoroughly they beat the cover as they contracted their circle. Towards evening they had some indications of success. Shots were fired, and some parties alleged that they had actually seen Seán and thought that they had wounded him. But when the twilight deepened over that place of gloom, all had to consider the day's work over and retire to *terra firma* without delay. The lord of the manor had invited a number of the gentry to dine with him that evening. Mounting their horses, they reached the castle after sunset. The day had been a strenuous one, wading and struggling through water, mud and undergrowth. Riding equipment was discarded and the company sat down to dine.

The night was warm. Windows stood open here and there in the dining room. Mine host sat opposite one wide-open window, but well back from it in the deep room. A tall candle stood beside him. Other lighted candles stood beside the guests. A musket ball passing through the open window knocked mine host's candle to bits.

A stunned silence followed. The shot had sounded well forward from the front of the castle, not from near the window. Mine host had turned pale, but was the first to recover himself.

'That was Seán Rua,' he said.

His voice loosened other tongues. There were many admonitions to milord to move clear of the window, some suggestions for the immediate evacuation of the dining-room, others for the pursuit of Seán Rua, vivid descriptions of the latter and of the ultimate accommodation which they heartily wished him. But milord, with a wave of his hand, silenced them again.

'The man who shot out that candle could, much more easily, have shot me,' he said.

And never again did he molest Seán Rua.

* * *

'Someone had blundered' by allowing the castle to stand unoccupied and in good working order while smaller mansions in less strategic positions had been destroyed. Such was the case, however, and in August 1920 the building was occupied by the Auxiliaries. They numbered one hundred and fifty men. All were ex-officers who had seen service in the 1914–18 war. They had been attracted to Ireland by the good pay, the prospect of adventure and the assurance of an easy discipline. I cannot say whether the rate of pay and the degree of discipline during their sojourn at Macroom were up to their expectations, but I am certain that they had no cause for complaint in the matter of adventure. For when the Truce of 11 July 1921 brought hostilities to an end, their casualties had reached half their original number.

Unfortunately for themselves, as well as for their victims, they added cold-blooded murders to their ordinary activities. On the evening of 1 November 1920 they raided the village of Ballymakeera, in the parish of Ballyvourney, in our area. One of their number entered a house where lived a quiet, inoffensive married man named Jim Lehane. He had just returned home after his day's work as a labourer. He was not a Volunteer and had no martial characteristic or inclination. He was talking to his wife while he filled his pipe. The Auxie asked him his name. Jim gave his name and the Auxie said, 'Follow me.'

The poor man followed across the road to the village cross and a few yards down the road beyond it. Here the Auxie turned and emptied a revolver into him at close range. Unsuspectingly, Jim had walked to his death. It was just a cruel and callous murder without the slightest justification, near or remote. It was only one of many.

There is a saying that a blackguard will be found in every crowd. The converse is also true and you will find a decent man among a crowd of blackguards. A small incident will illustrate this. One evening in the harvest of 1920, my brother Pat and I had come home. Dusk had fallen heavily and the critical time for a raid had, we thought, gone by. It was one short screech from brake drums that gave us warning. The Auxies had inaugurated a new technique to take us by surprise. Coming over the hill from the north, they had cut off the engines and slipped downhill noiselessly to our gate. They had already tried this method, but on the night in question they had improved on it. Stopping the lorries further uphill they had dropped a number of men who, passing through the school grounds, had surrounded the house on the west and north sides. We were now in a trap, since the south side was completely blocked by the high and blind wall of a neighbouring house.

The noise of the brake drums had found us in the kitchen talking to my mother. A bright lamp, just lighted, stood on the table. Very swiftly but silently we passed from the kitchen to the hallway, closing the door behind us to cut off the light. Guns in hand we went through the front door, which was open. Turning right we were soon at the corner of the house and in a small garden. Here we stopped. North of us we could hear men trying to get over the school wall, which had a coping of rough and pointed stones. To the west, and facing us, others were trying to scale an earth fence with a strong whitethorn hedge on top. We listened and narrowly watched the intervening ground where goose-berry bushes and small apple trees grew. Then we heard in a loud whisper from the gate: 'Georgie! Georgie! Get on with these men. Quick!'

Three tall forms approached us from the gate and stopped at the front door. One stepped forward from the gravelled path and onto a low wide step outside the doorstep proper. He knocked with his left hand on the open door, a gentle knock. Soon we heard the kitchen door opening and a dif-fused light fell on the three men. We knew that my mother had brought the table lamp with her to the hall. We heard her voice, speaking as if to friends as yet unknown to her.

'Good evening, boys,' she said gently.

'Oh! Good evening, madam,' a cultured voice replied. 'Are the boys at home, madam?'

'No, the boys are not at home,' my mother replied.

'I am very glad indeed, madam, very glad indeed. I am very sorry for disturbing you. Good evening, madam! Good evening!'

So saying, this decent man turned away and walked quickly back to the gate, followed by his comrades. A man like him is all too rare in the world, for undoubtedly he must exert a powerful influence for good, even on the worst companions. His gentlemanly behaviour most probably was the means of saving our lives, his own and those of some of his men. For, armed as we were, it is not likely that we would stand idly by if he were otherwise than the courteous gentleman we had heard addressing my mother. As it was, we managed to get outside their circle without clashing with them. We climbed over the garden fence through a narrow gap in the whitethorn hedge, at its junction with the school wall. As we stood on the fence our heads were just almost level with the heads of three Auxies who had climbed by way of a laurel tree in the corner at the other side of the wall. Another half-foot higher and they could have looked down on us, but a branch gave way at that moment.

With a crash they fell back in a heap into the schoolyard. We slipped off our fence and stole along the wall at right angles to the one they had tried to mount. The language we heard, as they sought to extricate themselves, and the energy expended on it, would, had they thought of it in time, have lifted them to any desired height.

The castle was a veritable fortress as far as our war material was concerned. Given a reasonable time and even a single field piece we could manage it. But we had neither gun nor mortar. Even if we had, we would have had to work quickly, since Ballincollig, with its large forces of mechanised infantry, was only sixteen miles distant. For that matter, every town in the southern counties could send forces against us at short notice. The brigade flying column, largely drawn from our area, never exceeded a strength of fifty riflemen. With the Macroom area included, our total strength would be about seventy, a small number, but high in quality as fighting men. Our heaviest armament consisted of two Lewis guns.

Elsewhere I have described some clashes between the Auxiliaries from the castle and the column. Our men had proved themselves more than the equals of the 'war-men of Britain'. In one engagement, which lasted for four hours, a section of the column combined with the Macroom men to a total of only thirty, had put forty out of ninety Auxiliaries *hors de combat*. The intervention of overwhelming forces of the British regular army saved the Auxies. We lost no man.

Ever present in our minds was the thought that one day we would return to the Auxies the compliment of their often inopportune visits. In other words, we were anxious to give them the pleasure of playing the game of war with us on their own grounds. Suggestions were invited from officer and private alike, and all were examined. The Macroom men were asked to investigate a legend we had heard about an underground passage between the cellars of the castle and the river bank. Such a gift was not for us, however, but we would be always welcome at the front door. Eventually it was the front door that was decided upon, if we could get that far.

* * *

During the second week of May 1921, the column left Bally-vourney to assist at the attack on a barracks in Kilgarvan, County Kerry. We arrived in Kilgarvan in the afternoon to find that the barracks had been evacuated only a few hours earlier. The Kerry men invited us to stay in the neighbour-hood for a few days, as there was a prospect of meeting with a strong convoy of military lorries. We agreed and stayed at a small village or group of farmhouses on the southern slope of Mangerton mountain. On Friday morning we had break-fast with these decent people. Then we sat with them on the low walls outside their whitewashed houses while the sun shone brightly. We talked of many things, but one old man always brought the conversation back to earth, to the land. He would like to go with us to the good land and fight for it too. The good land that had been taken from us. The land that would grow the big, strong men. That, he said, was the way to undo the conquest of Ireland, to put the people back again on the good land. Time has proved him right, but the wrong has not yet been made right, after forty odd years.

A local Volunteer arrived with a message. Our officers spoke together for a few minutes. Then our column leader called us together and told us our destination was Macroom, thirty miles to the east by our nearest route. We said goodbye to our good people of Mangerton and immediately we were marching. Keeping to the mountain, we made a beeline for Morley's Bridge, ten miles to the east. We enjoyed those ten miles over that high and rough ground, for the day was fine and the views of mountain, sea, lake and stream excellent. As we neared Morley's Bridge we had to cross a bog on a plateau hundreds of feet over the valley we were aiming for. It must have been fairly easy to access from some direction, for some of the bog had been cut away for fuel. The column marched two deep at a smart rate and kept step with precision. Our brigadier was with us and set the pace in front. I was at the extreme end with the Lewis-gun section. The column marched along the edge of the bank where the turf had been cut to a straight vertical face. The regular beat of the feet falling together and, of course, the combined weight of nearly fifty men caused the bog to shake. Presently I noticed a crack run along the ground inside the men in front of us. It widened as more men stepped on it. I warned the lads near me as the bank threatened to break away. Then I saw something glitter in the crack, on the sound side of it. I dropped on my knees to examine the object. It appeared to be made of bronze and a circular segment of it showed through the face of the bank. It was undoubtedly an ancient article and from the portion which showed I concluded that the entire object was a large bowl or cauldron. The topmost edge was but a few inches below ground level. Two of the lads who had remained now grasped the thing with me and we tried to tear it out of the ground. We failed, and we shouted after the column to wait for us. The column was halted, and our brigadier looking back at us shouted, 'What are ye doing there, Mick?'

'We are trying to dig out a piece of bronze here, Seán. It looks very ancient. I think it is a big bowl or a cauldron.'

'An ancient cauldron,' he shouted derisively. 'Some old poteen-makers' pot, most likely.'

So saying, he turned about and walked on. Snatching a bayonet I drove it several times through the mould to get some idea of the dimensions of the vessel. Then we hastened after the column.

Very soon we were dropping, almost vertically, onto the

little railway station at Morley's Bridge. Crossing the railway tracks, the road to Kenmare and the bridge, we turned left on the road to Ballyvourney. Soon we were marching on a road that led for miles uphill through a bare and rocky glen, our constant companion the wildly cascading Roughty river which kept on rushing down to meet us. The energy displayed by the little river and its refreshing music in our ears speeded us on our way, past that 'charming spot Glanlee', over the bridge at Inchees and uphill again to Sillahertane, where with regret we parted from our cheerful comrade the Roughty; he to turn right for Leaca Bán, while we kept on uphill for Coom.

We needed another companion since we had left the river, and the road to Coom was dreary enough. Soon we had him. Someone, thinking of the river, sang John Keegan Casey's song 'Máire My Girl'.

> Over the dim blue hills
> Strays a wild river,
> Over the dim blue hills
> Rests my heart ever.
> Dearer and brighter than
> Jewel or pearl,
> Dwells she in beauty there,
> Máire my girl.

Other songs followed until the top of Coom was reached. The rest of our journey would be downhill with the Sullane river from its source to almost where it ended in the Lee, just beyond Macroom. We descended Coom, passed along the valley through Coolea and Ballyvourney and halted at Ullanes for tea. After the tea I believe we could have cheerfully faced another twenty miles, but instead we rested.

The following afternoon saw us marching towards Macroom by the least frequented route we could take. Crossing the nearest road to Macroom at Ullanes, we ascended the ridge of Cnoc an Iúir and followed the old disused Kerry road along Ardeen hill. We descended through Carrigaphooca, crossed the main Macroom–Killarney road and, passing by the old castle, we crossed to the southern bank of the Sullane by the stepping stones. Upwards and to the south-east we crossed the third road to Macroom and passed through Dromonig and Brohaun to reach the southern road from Kilnamartyra to Macroom. Moving parallel to this road, we reached the hill of Sléibhín on the twilight. Coming out on the road, we marched downhill on its grass margins until we reached the castle boundary wall. Climbing over the wall we dropped noiselessly into the castle grounds.

Our scouts now got busy. Like shadows they came and went. We were led expertly forward, each section to its own position until the whole column had moved within striking distance of both the castle door and gate. A tedious and trying operation it was in itself, for, apart from the terrace, the ground sloped upwards in front of the castle. Except for a few distant trees it was entirely devoid of shelter. Without doubt, all available cover around the terrace would, in the event of attack, be scourged with fire.

The burning of a loyalist's house was to be the start of the first phase of the operation. His house was overdue for burning in any case, not because he was a loyalist, but because he was an active agent who nightly entertained Auxiliaries at his home. The house would be plainly visible from the castle and at no great distance from it. It was hoped that a strong party from the castle would rush to the scene to try to save the building and round up the fire-raising party. In that event we would take action. If a large party left and conditions looked favourable we would try to seize the castle itself. Let the party be large or small, we would seize the gate in any case and hold it against them on their return. At the same time we would keep the garrison of the castle indoors. Arrangements had been made for the Macroom men and a section of the column to attack outside the gates.

For hours we waited motionless, watching for that glow in the sky. It never appeared. Midnight came and with it the order to retire. We were never nearer mutiny. In vain we asked for permission to rush the guard at the gate and shoot up the castle windows as some small compensation for our crippled condition. As I picked up my Lewis gun I envied

Seán Rua an Ghaorthaig and his old musket. His single successful shot at the candle had also wrecked the peace of mind of his enemies and cheered him on his way up Sléibhín. He had made his presence felt, while we had come and were now retiring unknown to our enemies.

A plea for mercy had saved the loyalist's house from the flames and stopped our operation. Well, 'it blesseth him that gives, and him that takes'.

19

BURNINGS

It is still the same. If you come from the east the half-mile long avenue of lime trees will lead you there. You are at the Mills, Ballyvourney. The hotel where the stagecoach stopped on its way between Cork and Killarney still flourishes, though the stagecoach has long since passed on, enveloped in the dust of time. The old bridge which spans the Sullane is as sound and as picturesque as ever and, hard by, the Mill buildings are exactly the same, though renovated. And certainly the bloom of the rhododendron and the murmur of the river have not changed.

Behind the scene, however, some important changes did take place not so long ago. Up to our own time, Ballyvourney, hardly large enough to be described as a hamlet, was completely overshadowed by a unique feudal machine which functioned there. A high wall along the main road was pierced by the Lawn Gate, which gave access, by a short drive, to the Great House. Let us assume that one day in the bad old times, one has passed through the Lawn Gate on some legitimate business, say paying the rent. He notices that, a few yards to his right, another road runs parallel to his. It leads to the RIC barracks, which is conveniently near to, but of course not on the same plane as the Great House. Naturally, it gives him a sense of security to know that the law is behind him as he faces towards the buildings on his left. Soon the drive ends at an arched gateway. Beyond the gateway is the yard and rear entrance to the Great House. In front of it and to the left a gravelled walk leads up to the front door. To the right of it, a square tower with crenellated parapet looms up. The windows are protected by vertical iron rods, one inch in diameter, set in heavy iron frames, while iron shutters, half an inch thick and loop-holed for musketry, open outwards on heavy hinges. The basement is a dungeon with small, barred windows and stone stairway inside. An outside stone stairs leads up to the next floor, which is also of stone, arched and flagged. That floor is the courthouse, where justice, generally in small quantities, is periodically dispensed to the people of the district. The other floors overhead are the quarters for a garrison in times of emergency and were so used during the Fenian period of 1867. Truly an ensemble reminiscent of Torquilstone and the gentle Front-De-Boeuf.

It was the spring of 1920. That year had opened with a general attack on RIC barracks throughout the country.

Some had been captured and destroyed, some made untenable. The attacks continued and soon the British authorities decided to withdraw the garrisons from certain small barracks remote from centres of relief. Some hundreds of police barracks were evacuated and, on the night of 2 April, all burned simultaneously. Where the garrisons were maintained they were reinforced from the personnel of the evacuated buildings and subsequently by Black and Tans. In certain areas, where a large building in the vicinity of the barracks was available, it was occupied by a company of the British regular army. Our Intelligence gave us timely warning that the enemy intended to occupy the fortress described above and known as the courthouse, Ballyvourney. Its distance from the RIC barracks was less than a hundred yards. Once garrisoned, it would forever be a thorn in our side since we had not the means to reduce it.

Early on the night of 4 April, a small party of us quietly encircled the RIC barracks. We had little hope that the garrison would come abroad to investigate signs of 'riot, commotion, and civil strife'. They had long ago resisted such temptations. Indeed, over two years had passed since a Volunteer had, just after nightfall, walked boldly up the avenue and knocked at the front door. At that time it was a wartime regulation that a permit was necessary to sell certain animals. A voice from within asked who was there and what he wanted. The Volunteer gave his name, or at least the name of his loyalist neighbour, and said he had come for a permit. It did not work. Appeals and judicious threats about seeing the district inspector, an old friend of his, having failed, he was forced to go without having achieved his objective, the opening of the door. Other Volunteers arose from the shadows and followed him.

Now with the RIC barracks surrounded, another group got busy at their work of destruction. Large quantities of petrol and paraffin had already been hidden near at hand. Since we had no explosives to spare and the building was immensely strong, we had decided on using petrol freely. At that period of time the danger of handling such fuel was not generally appreciated. Among the Volunteers engaged in the operation, however, it was well appreciated. All had been thoroughly instructed on its dangers and the utmost precautions against premature ignition were taken. One hundred and twenty gallons of petrol had been sprinkled on the woodwork. In addition, several unopened barrels of paraffin oil stood on the courthouse floor. One was put in the dock for 'contempt of court' by the Volunteer on whose toe it had rolled. The commandant, with three men, was on the topmost floor. They had gone upstairs to open or break the highest windows to create an upward draught.

How the accident happened was never established. With two other Volunteers I was standing behind a wall near the gate of the barracks. A dull explosion, and the courthouse became a fiery torch with every window jetting flame. Other explosions followed as the unopened barrels burst and threw on fresh fuel. In an incredibly short time the floors all collapsed together, and only the thick walls remained. Stout walls they must have been to have survived the intense heat and pressure.

But what of the four men on top of that inferno? A figure approached from the Lawn Gate. It was my brother Pat, our commandant. I hardly knew him. His face and hands were terribly burned. He told me to get a doctor as the other lads were badly injured and to meet them at the old bridge. In a short time I returned with a doctor. He treated the injured and in a few days we succeeded in getting them into hospital in Cork city. All four had been equally badly burned about the face and hands. With the strength of youth and the spirit of the times on their side, they quickly recovered and were soon as active as ever. How they fought their way downstairs from the top to the bottom of that pillar of fire is a mystery. But again the spirit of those times was irresistible.

The burning of the courthouse had nearly cost us the lives of four of our best men. I believe the enemy did not get the slightest information that any accident had happened. While the operation was in progress they made no attempt to interfere with it, but kept on sending up distress rockets. A few nights later, however, they staged a counter attack. A party of RIC from Macroom, with one hundred and fifty of the regular army, surrounded our house at Caherdaha. They inquired for my brother Pat, who at the time was in a Cork hospital.

For two months previously, neither Pat nor I had slept at home. One hundred and fifty yards uphill from our house was a large barn. It stood on the roadside, a wide doorway opening onto the road from the ground floor. This doorway had no door. Inside were a few farm carts and some machinery. Overhead was a grain loft and there we had installed two large beds. For some time, three of us, Pat, Dónal Óg and I had slept there. Since the night of the burning, Dónal and I alone.

The one door of our bedroom opened through a gable onto the landing on top of an outside stone stairs, which was built along the gable wall. A wide gate mounted on the pillar of the stair landing gave entrance from the road to the open haggard. From the opposite gate pillar, the stone boundary fence of the haggard ran away at right angles to the barn. A short distance along it another gate, which we left open at night, led into a fruit garden. Diagonally across the garden a large sycamore tree grew on the boundary fence. Beyond were the open fields.

I awoke to the sensation of the floor shaking under me. Heavy blows from underneath shook me in the bed. They also created a noise that should wake any living man. It was pitch dark and I could not see Dónal as I sat up in bed. I could hear, however, his steady breathing as he slept peacefully through all the clamour. The light from powerful torches stabbed upwards through chinks in the floorboards. I could hear heavy rain blown by strong gusts of wind. The sound of these elements cheered me, although I knew that the enemy was upon us, or rather underneath us. He would presently be at our door. My immediate problem was how best to wake Dónal quietly. When a man is awakened, in the darkness, from a deep sleep, his first reaction is to speak and that perhaps loudly. I could now see him and bending over him I held my open hand close to his mouth, while I called gently. He awoke without a sound and I quickly apprised him of the situation.

We dressed quickly but completely, getting into the bed to lace our boots. Then, revolvers in hand we stole, step by step, to the door. Just as we reached it, the enemy arrived on the landing outside. Their torches shone through crevices in the walls around the frame and between the frame and door. The door was sound but opened inwards. The lock was strong, but its bolt went home into a thin square staple driven into the frame. The staple would be difficult to break, but it would either pull out or spring. The key was in the inside of the lock. I removed it gently and laid it softly on the floor near the wall. The enemy might see it, or feel for it, in the keyhole, or it might fall out and give us away when the assault on the door began. It was vital to us to keep the enemy ignorant of our presence until the last moment since they could, if they discovered us, riddle the floor with bullets.

The torchlights wandering around the door at length concentrated on the lock. Then started a vigorous assault with rifle muzzles on that region. We watched the bolt as it sprang back and forth under the impact. There appeared to be little danger of failure under that treatment. The small area of the flagstone landing outside restricted the number and movement of the attackers. They soon tired and changed their tactics. They used the rifle butts on the middle of the door. This method was a great improvement on the first. The bolt slid back much further in the staple, since the door bent in the middle, yet there was much to spare. Meanwhile the torchlight was obligingly being held for our benefit. It showed us the distance the bolt travelled in the staple and this was the measure of our time and opportunity. Again the method was changed and this time there appeared to be no doubt about its ultimate success. The rifles were discarded and men's shoulders substituted. Under their timed impact the door warped about the middle and the bolt slid alarmingly near to the edge of the staple. With each successive effort the distance lessened. I believe that not one-sixteenth of an inch was left between the end of the bolt and the edge of the staple.

'The big sycamore,' I whispered to Dónal.

'*Go maith*,' he replied.

A sudden silence fell. The last blow did not come. We moved a little to the left behind the wall. We expected a shot through the lock to break it. It did not come. Instead came the clatter of iron-shod boots on the stone steps of the stairs, as the soldiers descended. We heard them pass through the gateway and with others assemble on the road. As they marched off the rain stopped and the wind died down. I believe it was these elements that saved us by hastening the enemy's departure from the exposed stair landing. We unlocked our good door and soon we were hastening to the hilltop. The grey of dawn had passed. We saw the column of soldiers returning to Macroom. We came downhill again past the barn and with some caution approached the dwelling house. My mother knelt at an upstairs window. She had heard the rude knocking at the door, had seen some of the raiders search the house while others passed on uphill to the farmyard. She had listened for the shots which seemed inevitable, but meanwhile she had prayed to the Supreme Being who orders all things. That eternity of suspense was now over, the night past, the sun risen, the enemy departed and we stood before her. We did not speak for we knew that she still prayed, but we raised our hands in salute. Her smile was our reward.

* * *

Although it grieved us to do so, we did not spare the property of our own people when it became a military necessity to destroy it. This was the case with the Glebe House, Inchigeela. Our Intelligence had again warned us that it was about to be taken over by a company of the regular army. On the evening of 2 June 1920 we burned it. Among the local Volunteers who assisted at the operation was the son of the owner of the house. Before the burning a few Volunteer officers had started to break the news to the owner, by telling him of the impending occupation. He saved them further trouble by interjecting, 'Burn it, lads! Burn it!'

Three days later, Ballingeary Barracks, just evacuated by a garrison of the RIC and Black and Tans, was destroyed by fire. The two Volunteers who carried out the task did it to perfection, but, despite their extreme care, they got themselves slightly scorched. The physical damage they sustained was negligible, but they had to bear with fortitude the jokes of their comrades. For, having sprinkled the interior of the building, they retired the width of the street from it. They then hurled a lighted torch through the open door of the barracks. A tongue of flame shot back at them. It was bad luck indeed.

Once again, the enemy was forestalled in Ballyvourney. The Great House, fully furnished, had stood unoccupied for some time. It had ceased to function as of yore and had lately passed into the hands of a man of the people. It was regrettable, therefore, to have to burn it, since it was now his property. But it was absolutely necessary to do so. In a war one does not present the enemy with fully furnished barracks where he wants them. So on the night of 9 June 1920 the Great House ceased to exist. Its very walls have disappeared and the Lawn Gate gives access to the lawn. Here you may enter at your pleasure and sit and dream in the shade of the big chestnut. If a ghostly servitor, in knee breeches and claw-hammer coat, approaches and asks you if you have brought the rent, you'll know you have been dozing. If the vision persists, tell him that, despite the streamlined tails of his coat, he is out of date. He will then sadly depart and you may watch his progress around the drive to the gravelled walk. Here he turns right and, walking up into the air, disappears. He has just climbed the ghostly steps of the Great House to acquaint his lord and master that a mere Irishman without the rent in his pocket exists under the chestnut tree. If you do not wake up, a swarm of minions may surround you and bear you to the dungeon under the courthouse. Later you may find yourself in the dock of the courthouse, a bewigged judge on the bench, and a policeman or two on either side of you. You will note the needlepoint moustaches of the latter. Sentence is passed and you wake up with a start. The cold has saved you. With more or less hasty steps you 'brush the dew away' across the lawn and, walking straight through the Great House, enter the hotel.

The enemy won the next move in the game. Immediately the Great House was destroyed he occupied a fair-sized building a half-mile from the police barracks. During the remainder of the summer and early autumn this half-company of the regular army was very active. The RIC and Black and Tans did little. Both garrisons found it difficult to maintain their communications and supplies with Macroom, ten miles away. We blocked and trenched the roads, and, on a few occasions, roughly handled these elements of the enemy. Realising that the occupation of Ballyvourney during the winter months would pay very poor dividends, both garrisons were withdrawn at the end of the autumn. We did not burn the house which had sheltered the military, but we burned the RIC barracks.

Since both garrisons had departed, few precautions had been taken to guard against surprise while burning the RIC barracks. At noon on 1 November, two local Volunteers, Con Seán Jer (Kelleher) and Paddy Riordan were engaged in sprinkling the interior with petrol. The rush of many feet and a fierce hammering on the front door was the first intimation they had that the enemy was upon them. The back door was open and both ran through it to the yard at the rear. Con held an unlighted torch in one hand. The time was short but he paused, struck a match, lit the torch and, turning, flung it through the open door. The building burst into flame and Con and Paddy threw themselves flat on the ground in the nick of time to allow a regular volley to pass over them. Auxies from Macroom had dashed, in lorries, to the gate and had run the short distance to the house. Con and Paddy made another rush, running at a slant towards the cover of the Cascade Wood. A heavy fire clipped the undergrowth around them. A lorry had run up the road behind the wood with the object of cutting off their retreat. The Auxies dismounted and ran towards the Cascade Bridge, but Con and Paddy had just crossed it and, unseen, had gained the high ground at Ceapach.

We burned no house occupied by a civilian, loyalist or otherwise. The enemy burned nothing but private houses and property. In other areas, it is true that the IRA reacted to this destruction by burning loyalist houses in an effort to halt it. The enemy's burnings were invariably carried out as a reprisal for an attack upon them. They were both senseless and cruel. The victims were generally the occupants of the houses nearest to the scene of the action. Whether or not they were sympathetic to the IRA did not matter. They were ordered out of their homes and the torch applied. By this means the enemy hoped to terrorise the people and demoralise them to such an extent that they would inform on the IRA. It had the opposite effect. The people would not think of betraying the IRA, though the enemy did his best to provide them with easy means of doing so. I give below a copy of one of his leaflets:

During the last twelve months innumerable murders and outrages have been committed by those who call themselves

Members of the Irish Republican Army. Only by the help of self-respecting Irishmen can these murders be put a stop to.

It is possible to send letters containing information in such a way as to prevent their being stopped in the post.

If you have information to give and you are willing to help the cause of Law and Order act as follows:

Write your information on ordinary notepaper, being careful to give neither your name nor your address. Remember also to disguise your handwriting, or else print the words. Put it into an envelope, addressed to:

D. W. ROSS,
Poste Restante,
G.P.O., LONDON.

Enclose this envelope in another. (Take care that your outer envelope is not transparent). Put with it a small slip of paper asking the recipient to forward the D. W. ROSS letter as soon as he receives it. Address the outer envelope to some well-disposed friend in England or to any well-known business address in England.

You will later be given the opportunity, should you wish to do so, of identifying your letter, and should the information have proved of value, of claiming a REWARD.

The utmost secrecy will be maintained as to all information received.

20

SHOOTINGS

The Auxiliaries, the Black and Tans, the RIC and other terrorists of our time were not so nice in their methods as Oliver Cromwell, but they did their best. It was Oliver's invariable custom, before any fair-sized massacre or mass murder, to intone a lengthy prayer, not for the souls about to depart, but for propaganda purposes. The project over, this pious man stated a second prayer, its length in proportion to the volume of blood which had been spilled. On one occasion, however, he was known to have departed from his usual edifying practice. It was just after the siege of Clonmel. Two thousand of his psalm singers lay dead inside the breach whilst he and the remainder were still outside the wall and well back from it. Hugh Dubh O'Neill had beaten him badly.

'God damn Hugh Dubh O'Neill,' was Cromwell's prayer on this occasion.

It was Sunday 5 September 1920. The people had come

out from midday Mass at Ballyvourney and had scattered along the road westwards to the Mills and eastwards to the village. Two military lorries, coming from the west, threaded their way between them. The lorries were evidently returning to Macroom, having paid a visit to the barracks at Ballyvourney. The occupants of one appeared to be in an unusually good humour and smiled and waved gaily to the people. The other was a covered lorry, one of the usual type with light rainproof canvas on the top and sides. Having passed through the village of Ballymakeera, both lorries stopped at a point about four hundred yards beyond it. The spot was on a height, on open ground and commanded a view in every direction. Here they were out of sight for the time being. Then the children from the village discovered them and, approaching, loitered around the lorries to try and discover the cause of the stoppage. The soldiers made no effort to keep secret the cause of the delay. The covered lorry had broken down. They wandered about the road talking loudly about it and now and then cursing it.

The children returned to the village. All had the same story for the few local Volunteers they met. The covered lorry had broken down. The soldiers had said so. It could not be repaired. Some of the soldiers had suggested burning it. Others had said that it was not worth the trouble of burning, but to 'let it there to hell'. The last suggestion was acted upon. All the soldiers had mounted the open lorry and had driven away. The covered lorry was now abandoned on the spot where it had stopped.

Section Commander Liam Hegarty had got ready a bicycle to go on a journey when the news reached him. With Dannie Healy and a few other Volunteers he discussed the children's report. They did not doubt its accuracy, but saw the possibility of a trap. All were agreed that before taking the risk of a near approach to the lorry, it should be tested by firing a few shots into it. Had any firearm been near at hand the test would undoubtedly have been applied. Unfortunately, there was none within easy distance and they decided that, before it could be made available, the enemy would return to recover the lorry. It would be too bad if he found it as he had left it. It would be a disgrace. They would take the risk and burn it.

The children had again returned to the vicinity of the lorry. A few local Volunteers had strolled along from the village and had stopped on the opposite side of the road from it. It was their intention to give it only a few moments' inspection and then move on again. But their brief scrutiny revealed nothing and they lingered on, intrigued by the mystery and loath to leave without finding a solution. Meanwhile, Liam Hegarty and Dannie Healy arrived. With little delay Liam passed by one side to grasp the engine bonnet fastenings, while at the other side Dannie lifted a corner of the body covering. From within came a fusillade of rifle shots. Liam, whether hit or not, managed to cross a low bank which served as the road fence on his side. Then turning left he travelled in its small shelter for a short distance before he fell. Dannie dashed to the other side of the road and, gaining some scanty cover, got away unscathed. The other Volunteers and the children all escaped injury. A young man, Michael Lynch, lived a few hundred yards down the road to Macroom. Hearing the shooting he ran onto the roadway. He was mortally wounded by a rifle bullet. Whether the killers in the lorry aimed at him or not is not certain. But it is certain that one of the miscreants crossed the fence and shot Liam Hegarty again as he lay wounded.

What was the motive for this killing? The enemy did not mention any, but we came to the conclusion that it must have been a reprisal for recent attacks on them. The last action had taken place less than three weeks previously, at the Slippery Rock. Here one officer and ten men, fully armed, had been opposed to a fewer number of the IRA, only two of whom were armed with rifles. The British soldiers had been invited to surrender before fire was opened on them. The officer in charge had been killed and four men wounded, but there had been no unnecessary shooting. Some IRA men had come out on the road and exchanged shots with the enemy, and a soldier had struggled with one of our men to retain possession of his rifle. We had taken them as easily as we could possibly have done, and had helped the wounded to the best of our ability. The treacherous killing of an unarmed IRA man and a civilian, and the attempted massacre of others including children, was not far off the Cromwell standard.

Whether the motive was just a vengeful one, or calculated to inspire terror, its result fell very short of the mark. At that time the people of Ballyvourney, and indeed of all our area, would not yield an inch to tyranny or terror. On the day of Liam Hegarty's funeral they showed their appreciation of the man who died for Ireland and their contempt for the deed of terror. Behind the marching companies of the IRA came a mile-long procession of horsemen and vehicles. The Black and Tans in Ballyvourney, peering from behind their shutters, must have thought it interminable. The Black and Tans in Kilgarvan, County Kerry, where we laid Liam to rest, must have thought likewise. But whatever their thoughts, they did not come out to investigate the invasion. The barracks and the graveyard, both in the village, were but a short distance apart. Our firing-party's volleys, by a coincidence, were directed over the roof of the barracks. The Black and Tans must have heard the bullets whistle, for we used sharp ammunition.

* * *

The next shooting, the cold-blooded and deliberate murder of a civilian, took place in the village of Ballymakeera on the evening of 1 November 1920. Elsewhere I have described how, at noon on the same day, the Auxiliaries from Macroom had surprised two IRA men in the act of burning the Black and Tan barracks at the Mills, Ballyvourney. The two had escaped under fire from the Auxies after setting the building ablaze. The Auxies had returned to Macroom, and now, in the twilight, they reappeared in the village. One of their number entered a house, called out a married man named Jim Lehane, a man who would not hurt a fly and, taking him across the road, shot him dead.

Nine days later we lost Christy Lucey, one of our best men, at Túirín Dubh, Ballingeary. A native of Cork city, he had stayed with his friends and comrades, the Twomeys of Túirín Dubh, during the summer months. Having taken part in all the activities of the local company, he had decided to remain and fight with them in the coming struggle. Since the house at Túirín Dubh was practically on the roadside and well known to the enemy, he did not sleep there at night. Instead, he had his sleeping quarters at the opposite side of the road, high up on the hillside. He had established a routine of coming downhill each morning, crossing the road and entering the house. An enemy agent, taking note of his movements, could have reported that he crossed the road at the same time each morning. Possibly no such agent existed. The coincidence of events might have accounted for the tragedy.

As Christy descended the hill, his view of the road in the valley became more limited. He had actually crossed the road when the Auxiliaries arrived and, seeing him, immediately opened fire on him. He gained the shelter of the house and had ill-fortune not intervened would have got away from them. Immediately behind the house a mass of rock rose vertically. To provide for such an emergency, as was now Christy's, a ladder always stood in place against the rock. It had been temporarily removed and Christy had no option but to make a detour of the rock. This brought him again into the view of his enemies who shot him down. He was not armed. It was a pity, for it was a remarkable fact that even a shot or two exchanged with these warriors disturbed their aim unduly. A few weeks later these marauding Auxiliaries were trapped at Kilmichael, a few miles to the south of our area. Seventeen of them were killed. The IRA lost three men.

* * *

On 3 January 1921, five lorries of Auxiliaries from Macroom made a descent on a cluster of houses at Doire Finín, Renanirree. The raid was cunningly planned and viciously operated. The time selected was quite an unusual one, nine in the morning. The method of approach was clever. The main road from Macroom ran past the hamlet to Béal a' Ghleanna and Ballingeary. Another, the Leac road, converged on the former and joined it when about four hundred yards past the houses. The lorries could pass unnoticed on the Leac road, for, although near, it was under the level of the main road. That was exactly what they did. Then, having passed by the houses, they stopped the lorries, dismounted and came back on foot. While some converged on the houses, others crossed the main road and pushed on rapidly uphill to the north-east to gain the heights behind the houses.

The Auxies approaching from the front were seen and the alarm was given. In nearly every house there lived a Volunteer, but some were absent and the few at home were unarmed. Dannie Casey, a good Volunteer, whose house stood a hundred yards back from the main road, happened to be at home. With him was his young brother, Jeremiah, seventeen years of age. A box, filled with ammunition and gelignite the night before, was now Dannie's concern. He grasped the box to take it uphill with him until he could reach a place where it could be safely hidden. Jeremiah said that he would also go. Dannie told him that it was foolish to risk running away without necessity. Jeremiah replied that he had already met with the Auxies and that they had beaten him with rifle butts and otherwise ill-treated him, which was perfectly true. He was not going to give them the chance again, if he could avoid it. Seeing that he could not dissuade him, Dannie told him to go on ahead so that, if captured, it would not be in the company of a man carrying ammunition. Jeremiah left and Dannie with his box soon followed. His direction was roughly north. A quarter of a mile uphill over rough ground brought him to a point where he had a view of the ground which fell away in front of him to the east and north. Here he put down his box to reconnoitre and to rest a little.

Hardly had he laid the box on the ground when his brother and two other youths came down a short slope from the west. He spoke to them, pointing out the danger of thus exposing themselves on high ground, and advised them to avoid himself until he could dispose of the ammunition. They decided to drop into the low ground to the north. Scarcely had they gone twenty yards from him when a group of Auxiliaries rose from the ground to the northeast and fired a volley at them. The three immediately fell. Dannie concluded that all three had been hit. Seizing the box, he threw himself into a hollow due east of him. It was a shallow depression and he ran crouching in its poor shelter. Luck came to him in the shape of a mossy patch of ground under his feet. Parting the long moss, he found a hole just the size of his box. Quickly inserting the box, he rearranged the moss swiftly but carefully. It was well that he did so. He had barely straightened up and walked a few paces forward when three Auxiliaries appeared immediately in front of him. They ordered him to raise his hands, which he did. Approaching, they searched him. Finding nothing on him they questioned him, emphasising each question with a thrust from a rifle butt, while one Auxie kept prodding his back with a revolver muzzle. Several times they asked him what his business on the hillside was. He invariably replied that he was looking after his sheep. Tiring of the questioning, they started a minute search of the hollow where the ammunition was hidden. They diligently poked and kicked the very moss that covered it, but, fortunately for their prisoner, they did not find it. Disappointed, they resumed their interrogation.

Meanwhile, Dannie's brother Jeremiah had been borne downhill to his home by his two companions, who had escaped the leaden blast. Jeremiah had been struck by three bullets and was mortally wounded. An escort of Auxiliaries had accompanied the wounded youth and his bearers. By this time Dannie had been driven to desperation by repeated questionings punctuated by blows. He had made up his mind to snatch at a rifle and die fighting, but was always forestalled by the Auxie with the revolver. Of course, it was that gunman's job to kill the prisoner by shooting him through the back should he show resistance to the tormentors in front of him. Eventually, they marched him down to the yard of his house where they kept him under a strong guard.

Knowing that his young brother was lying inside fatally injured, Dannie asked to be permitted to see him. He was brutally refused and the beast who replied to his request thrust savagely at him with his rifle-butt. The blow struck him on the chest throwing him backwards off some steps. It is hard to have to record that a member of the human race should have been guilty of such conduct under such circumstances. It would be hard to describe Dannie's feelings while he waited for the order to march off as a prisoner while his brother lay dying within a few yards of him. At length there was a diversion. An officer arrived and called away all the Auxiliaries save one. Him he instructed to hold Dannie a close prisoner until they returned. They marched away. Scarcely had they turned the corner of the house when the Auxie spoke.

'Listen,' he said, 'slip in and say goodbye to your brother. Promise me that you will not stay long.'

Amongst the ruins of humanity, the kindly deed of a good man shines brightly. It is a great pleasure to record it. Dannie willingly gave his promise and saw his brother. He found him cheerful and only concerned for Dannie's safety. He lived to see his father and mother who had been away from home and who returned an hour later. Meanwhile Dannie had been taken to Macroom, to the castle.

The ordeal he had endured since morning had been a heavy one and it did not end with the close of day. It continued until after midnight and even then his hopes of leaving the castle alive were indeed small. Every now and then he was taken to a room where a number of Auxies sat around a table. Each of them, in turn, asked a question to which he expected an immediate answer. The questions circled like a point on a roulette. All were based on the assumption that Dannie was a member of the IRA and that he had that morning been on duty on the hill. Dannie invariably replied that he had been on the hill on his own business, looking after his sheep. It was evident that the Auxies sought to weary him by incessant questioning, until, through mental and physical exhaustion, he should capitulate. But they failed to shake him.

It is likely that, were it not for a diversion, Dannie would not have got off so easily. A prisoner was brought in, a young man on whose farm an old rusty gun had been discovered. On him, like mad dogs, the Auxies now turned their fury. Dannie, peeping through a chink in a door, saw and heard most of the horror. I will spare the reader the details. The British authorities announced another official execution. It was 'a foul and midnight murder'.

Dannie was released on the following day, in time to attend his brother's funeral.

21

RAIDS

By raids I mean the sudden descent of the British forces on the homes of the Irish people. It should be quite unnecessary to explain that our people had vast experience of these visits, in our own time and in every generation since the English first set foot in this country. The objective was always the same – the subjugation of our race. The immediate objective of a localised raid generally varied with the times. For instance, just prior to 1916, the RIC would appear with a warrant to search a house for seditious literature. After 1916 a strong force of RIC, accompanied by military, would ransack suspected houses and lands for arms. Later on Volunteers would be arrested and imprisoned on charges of drilling and possession of arms. Finally, for the two years before the Truce of 11 July 1921, the object of a raid might mean anything, even torture and murder. So common did murder, brutal ill-treatment and destruction of property become, that the people would not have been surprised at any form of terrorism. In the midst of it all, they saw the humour in any of these raids that did not have dire consequences for themselves or their neighbours. Enough has been told of the tale of blood. Let us look at the bright side.

It wanted a quarter of an hour to midnight in the late August of 1920. My father was reading at the head of the kitchen table, facing an open door from the hallway, while three of my sisters sat by the fire talking. One of them had just closed a book and had carelessly thrown it on the table. Captain Moss of the Manchester Regiment walked a trifle unsteadily through the doorway and picked up the book.

'Married in May,' he read, and added, 'regret in June.'

At his heels came a number of soldiers. His flying column of two hundred and fifty men had surrounded and occupied our village, the Cross, for the time being. My father continued reading while my sisters studied the fire. Captain Moss studied my father with owlish concentration. At length he spoke:

'Mister Schoolmaster,' he asked, 'are you loyal?'

My father looked at him over his glasses.

'You might have knocked,' was his reply.

'Are you loyal?' the question was repeated.

My father removed his glasses, folded them, put them in their case and put the case in his pocket. He got to his feet, moved back his chair and, moving clear of the table, stood in front of his questioner.

'Loyal to whom?' he asked.

'To His Majesty King George V of England.'

'I am loyal to no man,' replied my father.

Now my father was no fool and so far had never shown his hand to the enemy. While he never bowed to them, he never enlightened them about his feelings towards them. He liked to see a good blow struck, but did not believe in giving them the slightest indication of where it came from. In that, of course, he was only being wise. Now, whether it was the mounting enemy oppression or the rising tide of opposition to it that affected him, he appeared to have lost some of his usual caution. To my sisters, his attitude caused some little alarm, as they judged that the half-drunken and truculent captain meant to pursue his tactics further, which he did.

'Now,' he harangued my father, 'you have influence in this district around you, and I have lost some of my best pals here. It is up to you to use that influence to stop attacks on crown forces. And you,' he said, turning to my sisters, 'tell your brothers and your sweethearts that if a single British soldier is shot about here again, this house and every house in the village is going up. You understand that?' he said, as he turned and glared at my father.

'I don't,' said the latter.

'You don't,' he shouted. 'Did I not make the matter clear?'

'I heard you,' said my father, 'but if I had said I understood, it would have made no difference. It would not make you immune from attack on your way home tonight, or tomorrow or any other day. You must try some other method.'

'I'll try every method,' said the hopeful captain. 'I'll search your house for a start.'

'Do,' said my father. 'I cannot prevent you, but I'll watch you while you search.'

The captain glared again but said nothing, while my father picked up a lighted candle in a candlestick. Muttering to himself, the captain first selected a linen press in the kitchen. My father stood behind him while he searched the shelves carefully, starting at the top. He took plenty of time, and every now and then stopped to lecture my father. The latter appeared entirely engrossed in a study of the combustion of the candle, and ceased to pay serious attention to the captain's fulminations. My sisters were glad to see that his anger had given place to some other feeling, which might be something like a grim humour. But they never could have forecast his change of tactics. Little did they think that the 'man severe and stern to view' whom they knew so well and whom 'every truant knew' could be guilty of the childlike and reprehensible conduct to come.

The captain finished with the shelves and, muttering 'Not much there,' stooped to pull out a drawer underneath them.

'You will find that even less profitable,' said my father as he tilted the candle and deliberately ran a streak of grease from the back of the neck of the captain's tunic almost to the tail of it.

The tunic was very clean and new and the candle-grease certainly appeared out of place on it, but my father regarded it as an artist would a successful stroke of the brush. My sisters looked on in astonishment at what they first believed to be an accident, or an involuntary lapse on my father's part. They soon discovered that his employment was not merely temporary. Well versed in the mechanics of geography, he quickly added the line of the Equator to the Prime Meridian. The captain's portly figure helped him to a great extent. The captain's manner also proved useful, for while he intermittently lectured, a fresh supply of candle-grease was forming. By the time the searching of the kitchen was completed the meridians of longitude on the captain's back gave him a zebra-like appearance. As he passed from the kitchen into the hallway two Tommies with fixed bayonets stood, one on either side of the doorway. My father with the candle followed close behind. With wooden faces the soldiers faced each other standing to attention while the captain passed between them. Suddenly both turned their heads and stared after him. Astonishment was written largely on their faces. Turning eyes front again they looked at each other. Almost simultaneously both smiled happily.

It was not often such a blissful vision appeared to poor soldiers. The captain was not a favourite.

In the room across the hallway was a sideboard. While the captain searched its lower recesses, possibly for a bottle, my father finished his parallels of latitude. The sideboard yielding nothing, he stood up, walked out to the hall, looked up the stairs and, grunting an order to his men, passed out into the night. My father returned to the kitchen with his much depleted candle, to find my sisters laughing heartily.

'What's wrong?' he asked with forced gravity.

'Oh, nothing,' was the reply, 'but that fellow will come back and burn the house when he sees his tunic.'

'He's lucky if he does not go on fire himself,' said my father.

* * *

The dusk of evening, in the harvest of 1920, was a favourite time for a raid with the Auxiliaries of Macroom Castle. Two Crossley tenders invariably were their means of transport. The reader will say to himself that eighteen men venturing out thus could easily be dealt with. That was true enough, but the trouble was to catch them. There was no such thing as regularity about their movements. If they left Macroom in a certain direction the only clue to their return was that it would not be by the same road. Every kind of a passable byroad, as well as the main roads, would have had to be manned to ensure their capture, and passages thought to be impassable to motor cars were used by them. It was not for want of attempts to intercept them that they escaped so long.

It was one of these harvest evenings at the time when a raid might be expected. Mick the Soldier and I had just finished our tea, when the furious gallop of a horse sent us running out of doors. My mother stood at the gate. The three of us saw a rider ride a heavy awkward horse down the steep hill from Caherdaha. Stones and sparks flew from under his thick hairy fetlocks. His hooves tore the road as he was pulled up. The rider was Jim Lehane of Coolierach, a good Volunteer. He was bringing the horse to the forge when two lorries began to climb the long steep hill of Caherdaha behind him. Jim had urged the horse to the utmost, first uphill, next for two hundred yards on the level, and finally downhill steeply for two hundred yards to our gate. He quickly told us the news and galloped off. My mother went into the house while we went down to the Cross to warn anyone who might be in Den's pub at the corner or in Dannie Sheehan's shop. We first looked into the bar. It was empty. We ran out again. Then I got a notion as we passed along the front of the house. Running to the kitchen window, I seized the lower sash and raising it put in my head and shoulders. In the dim light I could see my Uncle Dan and Jerrick Sheehan, an ex-British soldier, sitting at the fire. Two full pints stood near them. Jerrick had been working with my uncle and both had just come for a drink after the day's labour.

'Clear out the back,' I said, 'and through the Brewery field!' They did not question my unceremonious order, but got busy. I noticed that while my uncle left his pint, Jerrick brought his swiftly but very carefully along. He did not catch the glass by the middle. Instead, he grasped it from above, with all his fingers around the top.

Dannie Sheehan's door stood wide open. Mrs Sheehan sat by the fire. Tadhg Buckley had just entered as we reached the doorway.

'How are you Tadhg?' said Mrs Sheehan.

'I'm the happiest man in the world,' said Tadhg, 'until I hear the sound of a lorry.'

'Tadhg,' I spoke sharply, 'get out.'

He turned quickly and made a dash through the doorway. Just outside was a large polished limestone slab. Tadhg's heels, to use a local expressive saying, 'went from under him' on the polished surface and he came down with a crash. Mick the Soldier found time for a burst of immoderate laughter, while Tadhg quickly regained his feet, and, crossing the road, disappeared over the meadow fence. We hastened along past Johnson's forge until we reached the point where the fence of the Brewery field joined that of the road at right angles. Here we left the road and slipped along by that fence on the side remote from the village. Reaching a certain point, we stopped to reconnoitre. We had heard some rustle on the other side. My uncle and Jerrick were just taking up a position with their backs to the fence and to us.

Jerrick spoke: '*Do bheirim ón diabhal*, Dan, I brought my pint with me. Ould soldier, boy,' he added in triumph.

A row of strong furze bushes grew along the top of the fence. Raising our heads cautiously, we were just in time to see Jerrick place his pint on a flat stone between two of the thick stems of the bushes. Then, turning his back on it, he leaned against the fence with my uncle. Both remained silent as they gazed towards the village, listening for sounds of enemy activity. Behind them we stood motionless, leaning slightly forward on the fence.

Suddenly, I saw something gleam in Mick the Soldier's hand. It was Jerrick's pint being carefully withdrawn from its resting place. He brought it back safely, turned towards me and, bowing gravely, raised it to his lips. I saw it tilt slowly and thought of Jerrick's care for its safe transport. I judged that a third of it had gone when it was again lowered. Again it was raised and lowered a few times, until finally it was raised for my inspection. It was empty. Very gently it was replaced on the flat stone and the operation was complete. Although taking no active part in the undertaking, I must get credit for not jeopardising it. For the struggle I had to make to smother laughter was indeed a hard one. We resumed our positions and waited, and soon we heard the noise of the departing lorries. Then my uncle spoke.

'They are going up Árd a' Bhóna, Jerrick, I think we can adjourn.'

'All right, Dan, wait until I get my pint.'

A clink of glass on stone and we heard: *'In ainm an diabhal,* Farmer, 'tis empty!'

'You must have spilled it, Jerrick.'

'No, no, I put it down on that stone there and there was not a drop spilled out of it. Someone must have drank it. It bate the devil. Or who could do that?'

A voice from the other side of the fence answered him.

'Another ould soldier.'

* * *

When British forces raided the homes of our people they naturally looked for some indication as to where the peoples' sympathies lay.

In many houses, prior to 1916, a large picture of Robert Emmet hung on the wall on one side of the fireplace. This was sometimes balanced, symmetrically, by Daniel O'Connell on the other side. A very poor balance it was, in my opinion. After 1916, however, equilibrium was restored, for a picture of the executed leaders was substituted for that of the politician. Later on, as the resurgent spirit increased, the pictures of other patriotic Irish men and women were added. Among them was that of Most Rev. Dr Mannix, Archbishop of Melbourne.

When a raiding party entered a house, the sight of a picture of Irish patriots did not tend to improve their goodwill towards its occupants. Very often the picture was torn down and trampled upon. This, in turn, did not help to soften the feelings of the householders for the raiders. As the struggle was intensified most of the people removed their pictures to a place of safety. They would be broken in any case and, moreover, their display would only incite the enemy to further effort and research which might perhaps reveal an arms dump in the vicinity or, worse still, a wanted man.

Our friend Seán lived on his farm off the beaten track between Kilnamartyra and Ballingeary. It was not often, therefore, that the enemy paid him a visit. The year was 1920 and most people had got accustomed to raids and searches. Seán was past middle age, stout, humorous and excitable. On this particular day he worked in a field at a good distance from his house and uphill from it. His neighbour, a young man, came running downhill to him.

'Seán,' he said, 'have you anything in the house? If you have, tell me quickly, and I'll dump it. The Tans are coming!'

'Oh! *In ainm an diabhal, na bitcheanna*,' shouted Seán, as a prelude to a quick mental survey of all the rooms in his house. 'No! No! No!' he added. Then, as inspiration struck him:

'*In ainm an diabhal! In ainm an diabhal!* Put out Mannix! Put out Mannix!' Again, to ensure beyond a doubt the safety of the Archbishop, 'Put him under a stone,' he shouted after the neighbour, who, to hide his laughter, was already speeding down the hill.

22

THE TRUCE

Looking back on the Truce with the British in July 1921, one regrets that it ever came about. For it was but the prelude to the Civil War in which we lost the best of our men, on both sides. That the Truce was brought about for that very motive I have no doubt. That the Civil War happened as a sequel to the Truce no one can deny, not even the 'wise men' and statesmen and politicians. I heard a prophecy made on May eve 1921, by a member of the flying column, as we sat on a big stone near Paddy Sheehan's house at Inchamore, Ballyvourney. He foretold the coming of the Truce, the return of the politician and a civil war.

We welcomed the Truce for its immediate benefits. It eased the strain on our people, especially on parents and old people, who waited nightly for the loud knock at the door, that forerunner perhaps of murder. Now they could sleep soundly, happy in the knowledge that their children were safe with them also. It was a great joy to us to return home to our people and stay with them, not for a hurried and fearful half-hour, but indefinitely. I well remember the first evening at home, the joy of my mother, father and sisters, and the neighbours who rushed in to welcome us back. For a few days we forgot everything in the delights of home. Then a dispatch came summoning my brother, our commandant, to a brigade meeting in Cork city.

Paddy Donncha Eoin, our vice-commandant, and Patsy Lynch, company captain of Ballyvourney, had come over on a visit to us. The four of us uncovered a Model T. Ford, once the property of the enemy. We found that, like Kempenfelt's ship, 'her timbers they were sound, and she would float again'. She bore the marks of some of our bullets, but none had penetrated her vitals. We started her up and found her quite roadworthy. About four o'clock in the evening we were on the road to Cork. We had read something about no 'provocative display of arms' in the Truce terms. Nevertheless, we felt that it would be a very uncomfortable sensation travelling unarmed amongst the enemy. We therefore carried our revolvers inside our trench coats. We wore our brown gaiters and boots and so were complete in the uniform of the IRA. As we approached Macroom we wondered how the enemy and especially the Auxies would take to us. It would be a new departure to meet and pass them by as non-belligerents. Our Ford rattled bravely down Pound Lane, and we would soon know. It pulled us gallantly up Castle Street, past the home of the Auxiliaries and across the square into the Main Street. Here we stopped. The three lads went into a draper's shop a few doors away, while I stood on the kerb a few yards from the rear of the car. Here I had my first sight of the enemy. He was an Auxiliary. Quite naturally, my hands slipped through the slip pockets of my trench coat and closed on the butts of my Smith and Wessons.

He came striding up the roadway straight towards the car. I knew, even at a distance, that he came looking for trouble. As the picture of a gunman he was the real thing. Very tall, well built and good-looking, were it not for a little bit of a moustache. This achieved the slightly sinister and military appearance he doubtless fancied. His armament left nothing to be desired. He was a two-gun man. His holsters swung far below his waistbelt and were strapped halfway down his thighs, in cowboy parlance, tied low. The riding breeches, putties and tunic he wore were well fitting, and the tasselled beret set off a handsome bravo. He halted in front of the car and gave it a general survey. Then he leaned over the bonnet and examined the bullet holes around the wind-screen. Next he walked around it twice. Finally he stood up on the footpath straight in front of me.

'That car belongs to us,' he said.

I said nothing.

'I said that car belongs to us,' he repeated.

'Belonged, would be more correct,' I said.

'It will be ours again.'

'That depends on your ability to take it,' I replied.

He looked me up and down. His hands rested on his hips, the palms outwards.

I watched him carefully. The guns were quite convenient in open holsters. It would take little time to get them out, but I had the advantage, for mine were already in my hands. Suddenly he raised his right hand and beckoned. Three more Auxiliaries crossed the street towards us. I waited until they came to him. They looked at him questioningly. He started to explain. With this advantage I turned my head and shoulders quickly. My brother Pat was just coming out of a doorway. I beckoned to him with my head. He came quickly, the others behind him.

'What's this about?' Pat asked, as he drew up in line with me.

'That fellow,' I said, indicating the elite gunman, 'wants the car back.'

The four Auxies now faced the four IRA men, ten feet apart. They heard Pat's question and my reply.

'Oh, well,' said Pat generously, 'you are welcome to it,' but he added, 'if you can take it.'

'Well, chaps,' said the fire-eater, 'will you stand by me?'

'Sorry old bean,' one replied, 'there's a truce you know. We were just going in across the way. Will you come?'

So saying, they turned away and, without looking back, made straight for the hotel. We stood motionless. The gunman held his ground for a few moments only. Then, putting his pride in his pocket, he started after his comrades. As he passed by the front of the car on his way across the street I passed by the rear of it. I could not forbear to fling at him a taunt.

'Well, what about it?' I said.

'Some other time,' was the reply, as he continued on his way.

We resumed our journey. Again we wondered how the next enemy group would receive us. A few miles to the west of Ballincollig we met them. It was a lorry of Auxiliaries, coming towards Macroom. They slowed down to have a look at the car. Realising what we were, they waved gaily and shouted to us. We waved back. That particular crowd was in good humour at any rate. At Ballincollig we got another friendly reception from the Tommies. Every group and individual saluted us good-humouredly, even the sentry at the gate.

Arriving in Cork, we got a great ovation from the ordinary people who recognised us as IRA men. The 'shawlies' and 'Echo' boys were especially embarrassing. Wherever we stopped they gathered around us. The 'shawlies' shouted to their friends across the street when in desperation we left one side.

'Look at 'em, Mary Ann, look at 'em! Ah, dere the lads dat knocked de stuffing outa d'ould Royal Irish and de Black an' Tans. More power to ye, boys, more power to ye!'

The 'Echo' boys examined our Ford, pointing out the scars of battle and weaving tales about its adventures. It had dashed through enemy-occupied towns, overturned barricades and knocked out armoured cars.

The outcome of our visit to Cork was the formation of a brigade officers' training camp at Coomroe, Valley Desmond. This lasted for a fortnight. Four men from each of the nine battalions of the brigade attended. The training was intensive and the discipline rigorous. We were routed out at five in the morning and until half-past seven were engaged at the most severe physical exercises. We then had breakfast. The same regularity was maintained all day at the various military exercises. We had four hours off in the evening and went to bed at half-past ten. After such a day sleep came to us quickly, and almost immediately after it seemed to us came Seán Murray's 'Show a leg'. It was five o'clock again.

The work was hard, but it made us strong and healthy. We thoroughly enjoyed our intervals of rest. There were good storytellers and good singers and good musicians to provide entertainment. But a simple incident or accident one evening caused more laughter than I ever remember. Now we had amongst us one officer, much older than the majority of us. We liked him immensely as he was a thorough gentleman, decent in every way and a good comrade. But he was ponderous in his ways. In his speech he chose each word with meticulous care and often used a heavy one where a lighter would have passed muster, with us at any rate. He always dressed correctly and never appeared without a white collar and tie properly assembled. Only in these small matters and *avoirdupois* was he at variance with us. But you may have often noticed in your schooldays, and indeed perhaps much later on in life, that youth treats age and weighty matters lightly. Now the day of this eventful evening had dawned fair and the morning had been very fine. But a fierce thunderstorm and rain burst over Valley Desmond and the 'thousand wild fountains' had come down and swollen the infant Lee to the dimensions of a lake which lapped and in places covered the boreen from Gougane Barra. Late in the evening the rain stopped suddenly and nearly all the lads cleared out for a walk. With them went our gentlemanly officer. Seán O'Hegarty, our brigadier, Dan MacNamara and I were left alone in Holland's kitchen. The training camp was being kept a close secret for various reasons and we had been warned to be ready to meet a possible incursion of the enemy. As the three of us talked together a whistle sounded down the valley. It was one of our whistles and it was repeated insistently.

'What's that about?' asked Seán.

'We'll see,' said Dan and I, as, picking up our guns, we hurried out.

Some little time before the whistle blew, a big horse with a cart heavily laden might be seen coming up the boreen, the only road to the valley. The driver was Jer Carthy. A most useful man was Jer. He was just now the mere driver of the big horse, but that was only one of his minor duties. It was he who had loaded the bread, the home-made cakes, the meat for tomorrow, the tobacco and cigarettes, in fact everything, onto the cart. But who had acquired them all? The same man. Who else could do it? He had done it daily for the column. Everything could be bought or requisitioned but the home-made cakes. They could be had gratis and welcome, but it would need a small army to collect them. Jer alone could do it in no time. Someone tried to explain Jer's system to me one time, but I doubt if my mentor understood it himself.

Dan and I went down the road at a sling trot. We hardly expected the enemy, but we knew from the whistle that something had gone wrong. Rounding a corner, we came on the scene of the disaster. The road in front of us was under water, and to the left of it and well out in the newly formed lake, the big horse's head only showed above the flood. A few of the lads had partly stripped and now stood perilously on a submerged rock, holding up the horse's head. Others were engaged in salvaging some of the goods from the cart which was almost under water and was tilted dangerously. It was evident now, from soundings taken, that an isthmus ran out around the wreck and that it was easier to work from the lake side. A deep hole lay between the horse and the road.

I stooped and started to remove my boots.

'Have sense man,' said Mac, 'there are more than enough on the job. The horse is safe now. We'll go back and tell Seán. He'll be wondering what happened. Look, the whole lot are here now.'

Mac was right. Men were fast hurrying to the scene. As we turned to go we heard a measured voice say, 'I have just thought of what I think is a good expedient.'

It was our portly and genteel officer. He passed in front of us and, reaching the edge of the deep hole, jumped into it and disappeared beneath the water. A gathering of flotsam halfway across to the horse had deceived him in the now failing light.

Everybody had paused, on hearing of the 'good expedient', to watch its implementation. Now, as well as I could see, it far exceeded their most hopeful expectations. It would need a medical man to describe their reactions. First, the audience appeared to be stricken with complete but short-lived paralysis. This gave way to violent contortions, followed by sustained convulsions. The group holding on to the big horse let him go and he started to drown again. They held on to each other and by this means managed to save their lives.

MacNamara took hold of me and somehow we managed to reach the house. Seán had come outside to meet us but we could tell him nothing. We staggered indoors. Seán now started to swear at us since we would not tell him the joke. At length I managed to ejaculate the officer's name. Seán heard it.

'Maybe he's drowned?' he enquired hopefully.

'Well,' I succeeded in articulating, 'he was under water when we left.'

Seán now became afflicted by this announcement. At length we sat on chairs and waited, our eyes on the open door.

By and by the procession arrived, headed by the victim. The mourners made an indecent scramble for position. They were determined to extract the full value from this unexpected windfall. Seán's face was as grave as the hanging judge's as his eyes assessed the depreciation.

'You got wet, Dick,' he commented dryly.

'Unfortunately, I did,' poor Dick replied. 'Visibility was deceptive, and I erroneously concluded that an island I saw was part of *terra firma*.'

'Better change your clothes, Dick,' said Seán.

'Yes,' said Dick, 'I will. A sudden immersion of that nature is liable to bring on pangs of excruciating pain in both my arms.'

'You are all right yet anyway,' Seán observed.

* * *

It was the harvest time in that beautiful year of sunshine, 1921. We had heard that my Uncle Dan was reaping the corn at Knocksaharing. Ever anxious to spend a day in his company at that peaceful spot, my brothers, sisters and I arrived there early in the day. We found that a goodly number of the neighbours, including the local Volunteers, had already come on a like mission. They had come, of course, to help at the harvest, but they also anticipated a day made pleasant by merely listening to my uncle's discourses.

Work was commenced on Páircín na Coille. It was the old-time harvest scene. Four scythes, wielded with precision by strong arms, cut a wide track from fence to fence. A taker followed each scythe. Two binders easily bound the sheaves each taker laid at right angles to the line of standing corn. Now and then half the binders would leave their work and stook the sheaves. Between the work, the pleasant intervals of rest, dinner and afternoon tea on the field, we found that time had gone by unnoticed. We had finished the reaping and stocking and now stood straightening our backs at the top of the field called Páirc na mBeach. Above us stood a grassy plateau with a lone pine tree in the middle of it. The sun, slanting downwards from the west, fell on the short green grass and cast a long shadow eastwards from the pine.

My uncle spoke: 'It is too early for tea, lads.' Then looking towards the tree he quoted:

'Come to the sunset tree,
The day is past and gone,
The woodman's axe lies free,
And the reaper's work is done.'

With one accord we all moved towards the grassy plateau and sat or stretched ourselves at ease around the stem of the pine. No one spoke for a time. I broke the silence myself.

'Dan,' I asked, 'did you finish your poetry?'

'No,' he replied, 'there's a little more, and it is very appropriate to the time and place. Here it is:

'Sweet is the hour of rest,
Gentle the winds low sigh,
And the bright gleaming of the west,
On the turf whereon we lie.'

Certainly it was appropriate. Above us a gentle breeze stirred the dark branches of the pine, while the sun sinking towards Béal a' Ghleanna maintained its pleasant radiance of light and heat.

It was but natural that our thoughts should wander back over that period of eventful years which had ended only a few months ago. Dan was the first to express his thoughts aloud. He laughed and said, 'Be damned, lads, do you know what it is, we have been through some stirring scenes during the past seven or eight years. If one could only think of all the laughable incidents that occurred from time to time. Here I am, thank God, back at work again on my bit of territory, I who was once a judge on the bench of the republican court, dispensing justice alike to rich and poor, bowed to and called Your Worship by the regular practitioners of the law, some of whom always thought, no doubt, that the dock and not the bench would be the summit of my legal career. Well, at least we can claim to have been the first Irishmen to establish courts for our own people since the lapse of the Brehon laws. And did they not work well? They never failed to measure out justice so fairly that the parties concerned were well pleased with the judgment. And what more was wanted? Soon you will see the British system working again, with some of the old outward pomp and ceremony. This was usually accompanied by, as we know from bitter experience, damn little justice for Irishmen. No matter! That can hardly happen again.'

The allusion to the republican courts, which had entirely replaced the British system, and which had proved such a complete success, evoked many amusing reminiscences. The judge of the district court was always a local man, farmer, labourer or artisan, selected by the people as the man best qualified for the position. His honesty was his only qualification. The court was held in the parish school or hall. The litigants could employ the men who had practised during the British regime, or call on any man they liked to defend them. Policemen and magistrates were local men.

It might appear to some people that such an arrangement was not conducive to the dignity and proper administration of the law. Such an opinion would be very far from the fact. The public were, of course, admitted to the court. The proceedings were conducted with the utmost decorum and a respectful silence was always maintained. This atmosphere was not due to the presence of policemen or other officers of the law. It was just due to the pride the people felt in the realisation of one of their ideals. True, if the occasion arose to justify laughter, then they had to laugh. But it was not done without ample provocation. In the days of the old regime the judge sat sphinx-like on the bench. His wig and gown gave him a most sinister appearance. Other wigs and gowns in a pit underneath him, uniformed policemen who glared about, the prisoner in the dock, the witness box, all gave an impression of unreality and unkindness. The silence of the court was the silence of fear, not of respect.

We talked of the evening Mikeen, the hard man of our village, had been tried by a special court. He had got drunk, assaulted a neighbour and threatened to blow up the neighbour's house with dynamite. He had assaulted the republican police who had obtained a warrant for his arrest. Now, he was about to be tried, but no judge was available. My brother Pat was asked to take the office of judge. He agreed on condition that Mikeen would be satisfied with his appointment. The prisoner expressed his entire willingness to be tried by a court with my brother as judge, remarking that he could now be sure of obtaining justice. So my brother Pat took his seat on the bench, for the first time I believe.

Public interest in the trial was great. The court (Den Buckley's barn) was crowded. Though the case appeared bad on paper, the world (of local people) knew that it had its extenuating circumstances. Yet the law had to take its course and the trial proceeded in the most formal manner. The usual good order and silence was observed. The 'state' evidence had almost concluded, in fact, the last witness, a republican policeman, was giving evidence. He was very precise and formal about the matter, in fact, over-much so. Mikeen, old soldier that he was, took advantage of the favourable tide. In any case, he did not like this particular policeman, who had arrested him, and who had just said, 'I took him into custody.'

'You did, you yab!' said Mikeen.

Calamity! But the people and court bore up bravely. Not until they saw the learned judge show grave symptoms of disintegration did they surrender. Then, led by the bench, they all laughed enough.

The sentence was light. The judge lectured him on the virtues of self-restraint and, of course, on the evils of drink.

Mikeen promised to reform completely, but the judge hastened to explain that that was not entirely necessary, that a
fair distance along that road would suffice. The neighbour
whom he had molested was then brought forward and
Mikeen completed his sentence by shaking his hand cor-
dially. Furthermore, he promised the judge that never again
would he interfere with the 'same man', a pronouncement so
specific as to be viewed with misgiving by some of the more
discerning among his neighbours. However, their fears were
never realised and ever afterwards they lived in the harmony
which began on that night when judge and prisoner, people
and policemen, all laughed joyously together.

The next case occurred in a neighbouring parish. The new
judge, a local farmer, had already dealt successfully with the
first two cases to be brought before the republican court in
his district. His judgment in each case had been applauded
by the litigants, the people and the lawyers. Naturally, like
all good workmen, he took a legitimate pride in his work,
and why not the same in his new profession? So far his
efforts had been crowned with success and a bright future
beckoned to him imperatively. But the course of success, like
that of true love, does not always run smoothly. Around the
corner will be found the obstacle, awaiting its opportunity.

The scene was again the forum and the third trial was in
progress. The great interest it had aroused was manifest in
the numbers of the populace who followed with respectful

and rapt attention the varying stages in the unravelling of its tangled skein. For it was a fairly complicated legal problem. At length, however, the full legal facts were before the bench, and nothing remained to be said but the pronouncement of judgment. All eyes were now turned on the judge. Very efficient and calm he seemed as he handled his notes. After a reasonable period of time he appeared to have made up his mind. He glanced upwards, then lowered his eyes again, and clearing his throat a little he said, 'This has been a complicated case, the most difficult I have met with, in all my *long* experience on the bench.'

The heavy silence was maintained. It continued long enough to allow the full import of the judge's opening remark to be assimilated by even the most dull-witted among the audience. And then the 'envious Casca' struck. Not from behind the judge's back but from somewhere amongst the edge of the populace. It was not a short sword or dagger he used. It was a high-pitched cachinnation. It rent the silence with cumulative effect. For it was possessed of that diabolical quality which compelled the listeners to genuine laughter in spite of their utmost efforts to restrain it.

Alas for the blight on flowering genius! *Olagón* for the glories departed! It is indeed a fact that people in high places must needs walk warily, and even the utmost circumspection will sometimes avail them little.

23

AISLINGÍ

What is it that has stirred the hearts of all true lovers of Ireland, in every generation, and has steeled them to do some deed worthy of recognition as a link in the unbroken chain of resistance to slavery?

It is the *aisling* or vision which only true lovers are privileged to behold. It is said that our forefathers saw it before they ever set foot on this land of Ireland. Since then our bards and poets have sung of it and have spared no effort to describe it. The Spirit of Ireland appears in the form of a woman, young and beautiful in appearance though of immeasurable age, and also known as the Old Woman, Mother of the Irish race. Her children are scattered to the four corners of the earth. In her hour of need she appears before, and her sorrowful glance rests on, some favoured one amongst her children. Sometimes it is at home in Ireland where the task she implies is comparatively easy, but sometimes it is far from it in a foreign land, alone among strangers or in the midst of bitter enemies. But wherever it be, whether on an Irish hillside, or deep in the gloom of a British gaol, or on a barrack square in India clad in the uniform of a British soldier, that appeal shall be, and has been, answered by the true son or daughter.

Neither time, nor place nor environment can intercept or obscure the *aisling* of Ireland from the chosen few. Tom Clarke was born in a British military camp at Hurst Park in the Isle of Wight, on 11 March 1858. His father was then a corporal in the British Army, but, like Tom's mother, was Irish born. A year later Corporal Clarke was drafted to South Africa, where the family lived until 1865. Tom first saw Ireland about 1870. His father was appointed a sergeant of the Ulster Militia and was stationed at Dungannon, County Tyrone. Here Tom grew to early manhood. His father wished him to follow in his own footsteps and join the British Army. But the Old Woman had already enlisted Tom in her own small but select army and at a time when prospects appeared most dreary. For the gloom of the famine and the defeat of the Fenians still hung heavy over the land. He was sworn into the Irish Republican Brotherhood by Michael Davitt and John Daly. He could have had no more worthy sponsors.

In 1880 Tom Clarke emigrated to the United States where he joined Clan na Gael. Soon he volunteered for active service in Britain. The ship he travelled on struck an iceberg and sank. He was rescued and landed on Newfoundland. Resuming his interrupted journey, he reached London, where he was soon arrested. He had been followed from New York by 'Henri Le Caron', a British spy. On 14 June 1883, at the Old Bailey, he was, with three others, sentenced to penal servitude for life.

For fifteen years and nine months, in the prisons of Chatham and Portland, he endured, without flinching, an incessant attempt to deprive him of his life or reason. This torture did not cease with daylight and recommence on the following day. It was maintained during the hours of darkness when even the vilest criminal was entitled to sleep and rest. But Tom Clarke and his comrades got neither sleep nor rest. Cunning devices for producing continuous disturbing sounds were erected over their cells. These are described in his book, *Glimpses of an Irish Felon's Prison Life*. The relentless brutality at length drove two of his comrades, Whitehead and Gallagher, hopelessly insane. With John Daly, they were released in 1896. Daly had been arrested a year after Tom Clarke and had hitherto shared the same prisons with him. Though kept apart, they had managed to communicate with each other now and again. The release of his friend was a sore loss to Tom Clarke, who, for a further two years, had to endure alone an even more intensified form of torture.

Released in 1898, he spent a short time in Limerick with his friend John Daly before returning to America. There, in 1901, he married Kathleen Daly, John Daly's daughter. With Devoy he founded the *Gaelic American* newspaper and, as its assistant editor, worked in New York until 1907. Then he returned to Ireland and opened a newspaper shop at Parnell Street, Dublin. It quickly became the meeting-place for Pearse and all that valiant company of a new generation who had also seen the *aisling*. They sought the help of the man who had for so long been tested in the crucible of suffering and had been found unbreakable. Nor did he fail them. Eight years later they repaid him by insisting that his should be the first signature to the Proclamation of the Republic. It was the greatest day of Tom Clarke's life, though well he knew it meant for him the end. He was shot on 3 May 1916. He was then fifty-eight years of age. Of these only eighteen had been spent in Ireland.

A man is judged by the life he has led. I know of no more splendid figure than Tom Clarke. The onset of the years chills the blood of most men. Add to this the incredible physical and mental torture which he had endured for sixteen of them. Most of the remainder were years of hardship and disillusionment. His father's influence and early environment militated against his faith. Yet, like Pearse, he turned his back on the beautiful vision of the world and set his face to the road before him, the road indicated by the Old Woman.

It would be easy to give many more examples from

amongst the élite of the followers of Róisin Dubh, as the Old Woman is sometimes called, but space would not allow it. Our own time produced many heroic men and women of a standard that could not be excelled. Some of the greatest came from the least-expected direction, the British service. I will mention only two: Roger Casement who returned a knight's insignia, and Jim Daly of the Connaught Rangers, who removed his tunic so that the bullets of the firing-party might not pierce his body through British uniform. It thrills one to think that such men belong to Ireland. Their bodies were destroyed in foreign lands, but their indestructible spirit came home to live forever in the hearts of their race.

There still live among us some of those who described Pearse and his comrades as 'visionaries', 'dreamers', 'rainbow-chasers', etc. They deserve no credit for their descriptive efforts, though they were literally correct. They forget that the vision precedes the reality. Their own vision was one which was very remote from the *aisling*. It was that of an ever-increasing bank account, to be added to regardless of the humiliating slavery which bound their country and their people. 'Stability' was one of their favourite catchwords. To gather up the goods of the world and live the lives of contented serfs, to fawn on their oppressors and to decry the actions of those who would break their chains, was its meaning for them. They called Pearse a fool, but he had anticipated them:

A fool that in all his days hath done never
    a prudent thing,
Never had counted the cost, nor reckoned if
    another reaped
The fruit of his mighty sowing, content to
    scatter the seed.

The Ireland which Pádraig Pearse envisaged has not yet been realised. It was an Ireland, 'not Gaelic merely but free as well; not free merely, but Gaelic as well'. Some progress has been made, but there is yet much to be done. What has been achieved was the result of great sacrifice and hard work by good Irish men and women. The ranting of politicians had no part in it and it is not to be expected ever will have in future progress. It is Irish men and women, educated to the true meaning of freedom, who will one day achieve it.

The *aisling* of the Ireland of the future, as seen by the greatest as well as the most humble among her lovers was simply a picture of the people, happy, prosperous and Gaelic-speaking, back on the good land from which they had been driven to make room for the bullock and the sheep. This condition once achieved, the prosperity of the towns and cities was assured. The old virtues, culture and pride of race would soon return. The politicians say that such a move-ment was begun soon after the Treaty of 1921. Its progress is not perceptible. The people are still in the waste places where they were driven to die, while the bullock and the sheep live on the fat of the land.

Our people must go up again to the mountain and look out over their splendid heritage and into the mighty past. There they will see an *aisling* that will raise their hearts and cause them to make certain resolutions. Some of these will be the resolutions of James Fintan Lalor:

> That of natural right, on the grant of God, the soil of Ireland belongs to the people of Ireland, who therefore have a clear vested right of property in the soil to the extent of full, comfortable, and secure subsistence therefrom, which never could or can be parted with, pass or perish; and which no power on earth, nor any length of adverse possession can take away, annul, bar, or diminish.
>
> That the people of Ireland have for ages been deprived of their natural right to property in their own soil, that their right has been in practical effect utterly defeated and diverted, and that it now requires to be asserted, enforced and established.

The all-encircling ocean is the boundary of their heritage. Let the thoughts wander like fleeting cloud-shadows over the land. They will pause, here and there, above the dust of our illustrious forefathers, and over that of the great men and women of our own time. All are now part of the spirit-world of the Gael, an invisible but potent force.

When we think of the past, we think of places like Tara and Clonmacnois, the two most famous in Ireland. Tara, seat of the kings of Ireland, was old when Christ was born. It was abandoned in the second half of the sixth century. Nevertheless, because of its ancient glories, it is still an inspiration. One hundred and fifty-three kings had reigned there before AD 563. Its traces alone, without the written word, give ample testimony of its former greatness. Four hundred pikemen of 1798 lie buried there. Their dust further sanctifies the soil of Tara. Clonmacnois, founded by St Ciaran on 23 January, AD 544, quickly became a seat of piety and learning and a city grew up around it. Students from every country in Europe attended its schools. Now it is a vast graveyard where rest the greatest and noblest of the land. T. W. Rolleston writes of it:

> In a quiet watered land, a land of roses,
> Stands St Ciaran's city fair;
> And the warriors of Erin in their famous generations
> Slumber there.

Other old places, pagan and Christian, next in renown to Tara and Clonmacnois, pass in review before us. Ráth Cruachan of Daihi, Maebh, the kings of Connaught, and the Tuatha de Danaan queens who gave their names to Ireland (Eire, Fodhla and Banba), all are buried there, not forgetting Conn of the Hundred Battles. Sheep and bullocks graze on this once mighty and populous plain. Cnoc Almhain, hosting-place of the Fianna, and Eamhain Macha, headquarters of the Red Branch knights, recall Fionn and Oisin and Oscar and Cuchulainn, Ireland's greatest warriors of the past. Uisneach, one of our most storied hills, where the ancient divisions of Ireland met. Once a great city crowned it. Here was lighted the first fire to the pagan gods in Ireland. Here fell Lugaidh Lámhfhada, one of Ireland's greatest kings. Here St Brigid founded a convent. Tleachta and Tailteann, old pagan meeting places famous for druidical sacrifices and the great fair. Nearby Slaine, where St Patrick lit the fire that quenched the fire of Tleachta and all other pagan fires. From Slaine our thoughts fly to Sliabh Mis, where a youth tended his earthly master's herds.

We pass over time and space to visit the mighty Brian at Kincora. He is mighty because by his energy and tenacity he succeeded in uniting the warring factions of his country-men and with one strong blow drove from Ireland a powerful invader. The death of Brian and the almost entire destruction of his race on the day of victory at Clontarf was a calamity not fully appreciated at that time. For, when the next invader came, a weak-kneed monarch occupied the throne of Ireland.

To encompass within a small space even the names of all the historic places of Ireland would be difficult. To enume-rate the battles, large and small, which, during the past ten centuries, have been fought on the sod of Ireland, would take a long time. To assess the amount of suffering endured by the people of Ireland during one day of foreign rule would be impossible.

I will mention only one more famous place, Aileach, ancient fortress of the O'Neills. Its age is over two thousand years. One of its chieftains was baptised by St Patrick. Out of it came the high kings from whom were descended Hugh and Shane the Proud and Eoin Rua. They, with their neighbours, the O'Donnells of Tir Conaill, will be ever remembered for the prolonged fight they made. Aubrey de Vere says of them:

Lo! these are they that year by year,
Rolled back the tide of England's war.

And finally, when Red Hugh O'Donnell had been poisoned and Hugh O'Neill forced to exile in his old age:

He sits abstracted by the board,
Old scenes are pictured in his brain;
Blackwater, Armagh, the Yellow Ford,
He fights and wins them o'er again.
Again he sees fierce Bagenal fall,
Sees craven Essex basely yield;
Meets armoured Seagrave, gaunt and tall,
And leaves him lifeless on the field.

There is a legend that in a cave under the hill of Aileach
a group of knights of the Gael stand by their steeds. All
are asleep, but only wait the word of *Síle Ní Ghardha* (Ireland) to spring into action for the ultimate freedom of their
country. Our gifted and patriotic poetess, Ethna Carbery,
describes Aileach and the sleeping warriors. I believe, with
her, that the men of today are as good as the men of the past.

> Oh, Síle Ní Ghardha, why rouse the stony dead?
> Since at your call a living host will circle you instead,
> Long is our hunger for your voice, the hour is drawing near –
> Oh, Dark Rose of our Passion – call, and our hearts shall hear!

APPENDIX

Original foreword by Daniel Corkery, Professor of English, UCC, 1931–47 and author of *The Hidden Ireland* and many other works

Where Mountainy Men Have Sown is one of the many books that have arisen from the happenings connected with our struggle to be free. Though the list of them is already lengthy, one still hopes to see it added to, in as much as there can hardly have been any wide district whatever in the country which in these years continued to live a quiet, ordinary life barren of memorable incidents. For memorable incidents, even visitations, were almost the rule. And nowhere were these events unconnected with the central impulse; an impulse which was itself long-memoried, long wished for, and therefore instinct with recollections of tragedy and exaltation. Why then should even one of our countrysides lack its chronicler?

Tragedy! Exaltation! – if only a small number of such books reach a fitting level both of style and substance it is not difficult to understand why it is so.

Few enough indeed. Yet the only books among them that one feels like putting quite aside, muttering *This is wrong*, are those which are written in an official-report style, laced all over with military-dictionary words and phrases, stiff with importance. It may be, however, that it is only those who lived through those years, who knew the leaders and men, and were acquainted with their views, who knew also the unpredictability of almost every incident that occurred – perhaps it is only those who find themselves putting such accounts aside as wrong.

This book, whatever its faults – and faults there are – has fortunately no resemblance to specimens of dried-out expertness. There may be unfortunate students who yet may have to study *them*. This book, however, the man in the street, and in the haggard, will be glad to know. For it goes its own neighbourly way. It is nothing but itself. That is, it is personal. From beginning to end it preserves its own identity. It is no 'report'.

To say this is not to say that this chronicler is a law unto himself, not tied down by the inviolability of facts, anxious only to keep the tale going passionately forward. Contrariwise indeed, we are on every page aware of a live conscience expressing itself. With his every statement, every expression we may not agree. 'This is too severe' or 'This is too flippant' may sometimes pass across our mind. But so to complain is not to decry his conscientiousness. As for his accuracy in setting down what did happen in any particular engagement – and the circumstances being what they were, always unrehearsed, haphazard, fortuitous, to remember quite correctly cannot always have been possible – if inaccuracies there occasionally are, they do not impinge on his probity.

One feature of his narrative especially commends itself to us – his feeling for the part played by the terrain itself. He describes it almost elaborately in his opening chapter. But having done so he is far from being finished with it. Naturally, of course, in the sort of struggle we are to read of – the few against the many, the inexpert against the professional, the clumsy makeshift against the perfected weapon – the terrain itself cannot but have been of inordinate importance – indeed its cliffs, its bogs, its streams, its track-like roads were all, of course, invaluable – and that objective terrain itself is everywhere in the accounts he renders us. But the phrase we have used is: his *feeling* for it. He is at one with it. As he makes his way towards some appointed hillside or hidden nook, the names of the rocks, the wells, the streams, the *cumars* he encounters seem almost to sing to him: their associations, their very dressings of moss, or holly, or basil, he almost fondles. It is obvious they always have been part of his consciousness, of the depths of it; one and all they cannot now but counterpoint the excitement that is possessing him. His observing of them as he passes on is therefore not at all a trifling with sentimentality. Nor is it either a display of scholarship, for such scholarship as it needs is also in the possession of his every neighbour in this Irish-speaking countryside. Those neighbours, as well as himself, with this terrain are at one. It as well as they are involved in this living struggle. And it is the decisive struggle that is come.

One other feature, perhaps, is also to be dwelt upon although it may be that it is implicit in what we have been saying. That feature is the historical allusions he makes use of. Many of them we have come on before – in books. Here, however, the book they are to be referred to is nothing else than the people's mind. One might almost say the mind of this rock-built, meagre, sparsely populated terrain – the mind of the Gaeltacht. So that when we come on some allusion which for us anyhow is not yet in any book, it does not stand apart from the others. The others it strengthens rather, makes them real. They remind us that the tensions that still stir in our depths are not due to the discussions of historians, but to the remembrance of very living local instances: the grabbing of territories, the laments of poets, the desecration of holy places, previous attempts at insurrection.

But it is rather with the way of this book than with its subject matter we have been dealing. The narrative itself is what really matters. It is full, clear, not over-written. It tells us of a small enough band of young men – the writer himself was hardly out of his teens – from Coolea, Ballyvourney, Kilnamartyra, Inchigeela, Ballingeary, who did not wait to be attacked. Usually they went out to find the enemy. Naturally the grown-up folk wished rather that they let him sweep by in his lorries and armoured cars. But even they, when the need was come, did not let the young men down. When any one of them was being hoisted to his grave, they gathered *en masse*, so proclaiming pride as well as sympathy. And when the young men's assault failed to breach the armour of the police barracks in Inchigeela, we read how the most respected shopkeeper in the village came to them beseeching them to take his whole barrel of paraffin to finish the job. Among the elders, such as he were not wanting anywhere. Those tensions required only the presence of the thing actual.

INDEX

INDEX

Lios Buí Beag 200
Liscarragane 188
Loch Allua 10
Lucey, Christy 125, 265, 266
Lynch, Con 202
Lynch, Johnny 60–70, 161–164
Lynch, Michael 263
Lynch, Patsy 136, 169, 200, 211, 285
Lyons, Yankee 141

M

MacNamara, Dan 290–293
MacNeilus, Donncadh 81–84
Macroom 9, 10, 12, 19, 33, 34, 38, 39,
    43, 46, 73, 81, 86, 89, 100, 101,
    107, 108, 114, 115, 128, 131, 133,
    137, 141, 143, 147, 161, 168, 169,
    172, 174, 175, 177, 188, 199, 203,
    205, 207–210, 228–240, 243, 244,
    250, 254, 257, 261, 263, 265, 266,
    270, 277, 285, 288
Mac Suibhne, Éamon 7
MacSweeney, Dan T. 62, 64, 66, 67
MacSweeney, John McCann 125, 169
Maher, Fr Michael 79
Mangerton 239, 240
Maoileann 158
Markievicz, Countess 78
Millstreet 11, 37, 177–179
Morley's Bridge 240, 242
Moss, Captain 273
Moynihan, Jack 125
Moynihan, Jamie 62, 64, 66, 67,
    93–95, 119, 139
Muing 223
Muing Lia 178
Muing na Biorraí 20, 70
Múirneach Beag 7
Murphy, Mick 186, 191
Murray, Pat 125
Murray, Seán 169, 185–187, 189, 289
Murray, Tom 168
Muskerry 18, 19

N

Na hInseacha 19

National Volunteers 32, 33
Neville, Neddy 174

O

O'Brien, Master M. (Ó Briain,
    Micheál) 120–122
O'Connell, Mick (the Soldier)
    112–114, 116, 119, 131, 138–140,
    278–280
O'Connell, Neilus (Louth) 71–73,
    80, 81, 112–114
O'Connell, Terry 114
O'Donohue, Fr 34
O'Growney, Fr 30
O'Hegarty, Seán 176, 185, 240, 241,
    290, 292, 293
Ó Laoghaire, Barra 19
O'Leary, Dan Thade Seáin 125
Ó Luingsigh, Amhlaoibh 19
Ó Súilleabháin, Pat 33, 38, 42, 51, 52,
    57, 58, 62, 80, 81, 97, 103–105,
    109, 112–114, 117, 118, 120, 159,
    169, 170, 178, 180, 185, 200, 211,
    235, 250, 251, 285, 287, 297, 298
Ó Súilleabháin, Patsy 143–145, 150
O'Sullivan, Corney 169, 181,
    185–187, 190, 200, 211, 212
O'Sullivan, Dan 124, 125
O'Sullivan, Eugene (Hugie) 169,
    170, 175, 185–187
O'Sullivan, Jerry (Conch) 115
O'Sullivan, Paddy Donncha Eoin
    133, 136, 138, 200, 211, 285
O'Sullivan, Seánín Donncha Eoin
    131–133

P

Paps mountains 214
Pearse, Pádraig 27, 30, 43, 304–306
Percival, Major 225–227
Poul na Bró 47, 120, 132, 133, 181,
    182, 213, 216, 225
Poul na Circe 60

Q

Quill, John J. 225

319